Headline News Discussion Starters

From the Editors
of Group Publishing

Loveland, Colorado

Headline News Discussion Starters
Copyright © 1990 by Group Publishing, Inc.

First Printing

All rights reserved. The Discussion Starters in this book may be reproduced without permission from the publisher for their intended use in local churches only. The material may not, however, be used or reproduced in other books or publications without prior permission from the publisher. For information write Permissions, Group Books, Box 481, Loveland, CO 80539.

Credits
Edited by Stephen P. Parolini
Designed by Judy Atwood Bienick
Illustrations by Judy Atwood Bienick

Scripture quotations are from the Holy Bible, New International Version. Copyright ©1973, 1978, 1984 International Bible Society. Used by permission of Zondervan Bible Publishers.

Library of Congress Cataloging-in-Publication Data
Headline news discussion starters / compiled by Group Books.
    p.   cm.
    ISBN 1-55945-000-2
    1. Church group work with teenagers 2. Church and social problems—United States.
3. United States—Moral conditions. I. Group Books (Firm)
BV4447.H34   1990
261.8—dc20   89-77832
                                                                                    CIP

Printed in the United States of America

CONTENTS

Introduction 5

SECTION ONE: Ethics

National Experts Debate Legalization of Drugs 8
Sheriff Offers Reward to Stop Teenage Drinking 10
Black Best Man Barred From Wedding by Church 12
Two Thefts Prompted by Hunger and Sickness 14
Medical Experts Oppose Animal Experimentation...............16
Motorists Keep Money Found on Interstate........................18
NASA Plans to Spend Billions on Exploration....................20

SECTION TWO: Religion

Woman Refuses to Work on Sabbath; Gets Fired 24
Man Claims to Spend Five Days in Heaven 26
Minor Evangelist's Tour Makes Major Money 28
Woman Says Prayer Helped Her Win Lottery 30
Church Member Shares Beer With Teenagers 32
Woman Faces Jail for Taking Kids to Church......................34
Woman Dies From Fast...36

SECTION THREE: School

Student Test Canceled After Answers Published.................40
Principal Has Teacher Change Athlete's Grade 42
Professor Requires Students to Risk Failure 44
Teacher Expects Too Much of His Students 46
High School Yearbook Publishes Racial Slur 48
Teenager Says Her Figure Nixed Her Cheerleading.............50
Black Principal Faces Problems and Prejudice....................52
Teenage Tycoons Find Success in Business........................54

SECTION FOUR: Sexuality

Abortion Pill Raises New Birth Control Questions 58
Christians Debate Teen Use of Birth Control 60
School May Suspend Kids for Public Affection 62
Reverend Distributes Condoms in Church 64
Special School for Gay Kids Sparks Controversy 66
Sex Ads Bring Big Bucks 68

SECTION FIVE: Law and Violence

Boyfriend Burns House; Four People Die in Fire 72
Father Shot; Children Charged With Murder 74
Weapons Discovered in Schools; Kids Arrested 76
Christians Arrested for Abortion Clinic Bombings 78
New Law Would Punish Parents for Kids' Crimes 80
Killer of Homosexuals Given Light Sentence 82
Mother Arrested for Humiliating Her Child 84

SECTION SIX: Unusual Stories

Elvis Worshiped by Fans 88
Report Claims Men Can Now Become Pregnant 90
Company Helps People Get Even With Enemies 92
Couple Married After They Die in Plane Crash 94
Fake Slings and Neck Braces Gain Sympathy 96

Introduction

"Woman Refuses to Work on Sabbath; Gets Fired"

"Father Shot; Children Charged With Murder"

"Man Claims to Spend Five Days in Heaven"

"Report Claims Men Can Now Become Pregnant"

Today's newspaper and magazine headlines go from mildly interesting to surprising. The stories often shock, startle or intrigue readers. And many are controversial. The same story, read by two different people, might prompt such diverse reactions as "He got what he deserved" and "I can't believe they did that to him."

Controversy makes for great discussion.

And great discussion is what this book is all about. *Headline News Discussion Starters* is a collection of actual newspaper and magazine stories that will challenge your teenagers to think about such issues as racism, religious rights, AIDS and more. Each article is followed by Discussion Starters filled with thoughtful and probing questions designed to help kids see how the topic relates to their faith. Discussion Starters also include scripture verses to help teenagers see what the Bible says about the topic. Some of the articles have additional activities for kids to complete and discuss. The articles have been adapted from the World Times section of GROUP Magazine.

The 40 articles and Discussion Starters can be used in a number of different ways. Just photocopy the article you need and you're ready to go. Use the articles to begin youth group meetings. Have teenagers lead their own weekly discussions using the book as a guide. Plan a retreat around the theme of "Headline News Discussion Starters" and add your own creative activities to the questions provided. Use the book in Sunday school. Or have teenagers use articles to spark discussion with parents about the topics.

Headline News Discussion Starters will challenge your teenagers to think through tough issues. And it will help them turn interesting news stories into relevant discussion—discussion that can have a positive impact on their Christian growth.

SECTION ONE:
Ethics

National Experts Debate Legalization of Drugs

NEW YORK—Pointing to the rising cost of fighting illegal drug use, many influential American leaders are saying it's time to legalize some or all drugs. Supporters say making drugs such as marijuana, heroin and cocaine legal will cut down on prison overcrowding, violence in urban areas and shaky international relations with drug-exporting countries such as Panama.

New York criminologist Georgette Bennett said: "There is no question we have a very big drug problem in this country. The question is: Is our current policy the best way to deal with it? My answer is no: By making drugs a criminal matter, we have in fact made the problem worse. If we decriminalize, at least we would only have a massive public-health problem on our hands, instead of a massive crime problem, a massive corruption problem and a massive foreign-policy problem."

Bennett is not alone in her recommendation. Columnist William F. Buckley Jr., Nobel-prize-winner economist Milton Friedman, and U.S. Representatives Fortney Stark of California and Steny Hoyer of Maryland are among those who support legalization in some form. They advocate taxing the sale of drugs and using the money for anti-drug campaigns and rehabilitation.

But those who disagree say that legalization would touch off a catastrophic rise in drug abuse. Robert DuPont, former head of the National Institute on Drug Abuse, believes the potential market for legalized drugs is comparable to the number of Americans who now use alcohol—140 million people. He says up to 50 million people would eventually use cocaine, with 10 million of those hard-core addicts. New York Senator Alfonse D'Amato said legalization is immoral and would turn the U.S. into "a society of zombies."

Discussion Starters

● Is drug abuse a criminal problem or a public health problem? Explain. Is drug abuse contrary to God's will? Why or why not? Why should marijuana and cocaine be illegal when alcohol and tobacco, two drugs that account for more than 400,000 deaths each year, are legal? When the prohibition against alcohol was lifted in the late 1920s, bootleggers soon went out of business. Do you think the same thing would happen to drug dealers if drugs were legalized? Why or why not?

● Is it a sin to use drugs if the user doesn't hurt anyone else? Why or why not? If drugs are legalized, do you think we'll become "a society of zombies," or will the drug problem decrease? Explain.

● Read Romans 14:14-23. What does Paul mean when he says "no food is unclean in itself"? Is an illegal drug "unclean" or evil in itself? Why or why not? Paul says to not cause your neighbor to stumble by what you eat or drink. How can using illegal drugs cause the user's neighbors to stumble?

● Read Romans 13:1-7. What can the government dictate about what you do to your own body? If the government decides to legalize drugs, are you free to experiment? Why or why not? Read Galatians 3:22-24. What's the purpose of a just law?

● Read 1 Corinthians 3:16-17. Name five things that build up your body as a temple of God. Name five things that tear it down. How would drug use affect your "temple"? If God views your body as his house, how do you think God feels about drug use? Explain.

Sheriff Offers Reward to Stop Teenage Drinking

FORT COLLINS, Colo.—In an effort to curb underage drinking, Larimer County Sheriff Jim Black is offering $50 to anyone with information about beer keg parties that involve minors.

"This kind of [beer drinking] activity seems to occur in most communities across the country," says Black, "and we're going to try to stop it in Larimer County. We are adopting a zero-tolerance policy."

The cash reward will be given to anyone contacting the Sheriff's Department with information about any underage drinking party of 30 people or more. If minors are present at the party, they will be detained until their parents pick them up. Also, Black says adults who sponsor a keg party with underage drinkers attending will be arrested and charged with contributing to the delinquency of a minor.

"When you're in high school, you start to build your life," says Black. "Just when youths are ready to begin a new life, often they go to a keg party and tragically end their lives on the way home."

Fort Collins High School Principal John Longtin says: "The key focus is protecting young people. And when lives are at stake, we all have a vested interest and responsibility particularly when it comes to young lives."

Informants will remain anonymous, says Black. Each informant will choose a four-digit code and use the code to collect the reward.

Discussion Starters

● If Sheriff Black's anti-drinking program was in your area, would you let the Sheriff's Department know about beer parties that serve underage young people? Why or why not? How well do you think the anti-drinking program will cut down on the number of beer parties? Explain.

● Read Romans 14:10-13. If you tell the authorities about an illegal beer party, are you judging the people who go to the party? Why or why not? If you don't stop someone from doing something wrong, how are you a stumbling block to that person?

● Read Proverbs 20:1; Romans 13:12-14; and Ephesians 5:17-21. How do you feel about attending a beer party? Is it okay to drink as long as you don't get drunk? Why or why not? What's the best reason you know to not get drunk? What can a relationship with God give you that alcohol can't?

● Read 1 John 4:20-21. Is it a loving thing to tell the police about an underage drinking party? Why or why not? What's the best way to show your love for someone you know who's planning to go to a beer party?

● Read Titus 3:1-2. If you know about a beer party that some underage people are attending, is it a sin to keep that information to yourself? Why or why not? What's the main reason we're asked to obey the authorities in our society?

● Read 2 Samuel 12:1-15. Why is it hard to confront someone who's done something wrong? Is it okay to confront someone who's doing the same thing you've done in the past? Why or why not?

Black Best Man Barred From Wedding by Church

KISSIMMEE, Fla.—A young white couple canceled their wedding plans after they learned that their best man wouldn't be allowed in the church. Their best man is black.

John Hill, 18, and his fiancee, Lori Hodges, also 18, planned to be married in Emmanuel Baptist Church, pastored by Rev. Horace Burgner.

"I didn't know he had to know the color of my wedding party. He said, 'John, I can't do it. My church is segregated.'" said Hill.

"I almost hung up on him. It shocked all of us. My guests deserve to be treated better than that."

Burgner denied a charge that he or his church are racist. "I have a lot of colored friends," he said. "We don't believe in looking down our noses at any other races but we believe in segregation of races as taught by God in the Bible."

Discussion Starters

● What would you do if you were John or Lori? What would you say to Rev. Burgner?

● Should God punish Rev. Burgner for his beliefs? If so, what should be the punishment? If not, why not?

● How do you know whether or not you're a racist? What makes someone a racist? How do you think God will judge you if you're a Christian and haven't done anything to stop racial injustice? Explain.

● If you don't know any people from other races, are you a racist? Why do you suppose most white Christians have little contact with people of other races? Does that make them racist? Explain.

● Read Matthew 10:5. Was Jesus a racist? Read John 4:7-9. Discuss.

● What stereotypes do people in your group have of different races? What stereotypes do people of other races have of your race? What's the danger in stereotyping races?

● Read Leviticus 25:44-45 and Deuteronomy 23:3. Are Rev. Burgner's actions justified? Should we associate only with people from our own race, as these passages indicate? Read Galatians 3:27-28. What should you do when Bible passages seem to contradict each other? How do you know which passage is valid for you? Discuss.

● Is it okay to go to an all-white, all-black or all-Hispanic church? Why or why not?

● Are minorities oppressed in America? Explain.

● How involved should the government be in regulating religious practices? Were the best man's rights violated even though the church isn't under state regulation? Explain.

● Read 1 Corinthians 13:4-7. How can you show love to people of other races?

Two Thefts Prompted by Hunger and Sickness

Seventeen-year-old Horacio Rosas Donjuan Jr. of Pasadena, Texas, was sentenced to a month in jail for stealing two pears from a neighbor's refrigerator. Donjuan was hungry, said a prosecutor.

The teenager was sentenced to a month in jail and a year's probation, plus he had to return to school after his release.

Meanwhile, a Denver man, Robert Jaramillo, 29, says he burglarized a business to get money for treatment for his fatally sick daughter. Jaramillo was arrested when he decided not to complete the theft and was returning the calculators to the store shelf.

Jaramillo was placed on unsupervised probation for two years. According to the district attorney, "It's unusual for someone charged with burglary to get a deferred judgment. But the circumstances surrounding the child were probably the motivation for the crime." Jaramillo's charges will be dropped if he doesn't violate any laws during this probation.

Is It Ever Okay?

Is it ever okay to disobey one of the Ten Commandments? Read each Bible passage listed. Then, for each, check the appropriate column. If you check "Could be okay to disobey" or "Always okay to disobey," write an example. Discuss your answers.

Bible Passage	Never okay to disobey	Could be okay to disobey	Always okay to disobey
Exodus 20:2-3			
Exodus 20:4-6			
Exodus 20:7			
Exodus 20:8-11			
Exodus 20:12			
Exodus 20:13			
Exodus 20:14			
Exodus 20:15			
Exodus 20:16			
Exodus 20:17			

Discussion Starters

● Was Donjuan's sentence too lenient? too tough? Explain.

● Was Jaramillo's sentence too lenient? too tough? Explain.

● The district attorney in Jaramillo's case said the circumstances were probably the motivation for the crime. Is wanting to treat sickness a good reason for crime? Why or why not? Is wanting to eat a good reason for crime? Why or why not?

● If you were Donjuan or Jaramillo, what would you have done? What would have been alternatives to stealing? If a person has a good reason to steal, is it okay? Or is stealing wrong, no matter what? Explain.

● Read Mark 3:1-5. Why did Jesus break a law? If an action will do good—even if it's against a law—is it okay? Why or why not? Does that mean Donjuan and Jaramillo were justified in breaking the law? Explain.

● Read Matthew 22:36-40. How would you act if the loving thing to do were illegal? Give examples of times when love might make you consider breaking a law; for example, speeding to get to a depressed friend sooner. Give examples of times when love might keep you from doing something that's legal; for example, getting an abortion.

● Do the "Is It Ever Okay?" box. What's a time when you felt you had good reason to do something against the law? How can you make decisions about obeying or disobeying the Ten Commandments? the laws of your country? your rules at home?

Medical Experts Oppose Animal Experimentation

NEW YORK—A female rhesus monkey, her infant clinging to her breast, flits about a cage at a New York University Medical Center facility.

Once the baby is weaned, the mother will undergo brain surgery to give her Parkinson's disease. Then she will receive either fetal cell implants or drug therapies to see whether she—and possibly humans—can be cured of this chronic progressive condition that leaves its victims with tremors and muscle weakness.

For many medical researchers, and most of the public, medical advances made through animal experimentation are acceptable.

But animal rights activists disagree.

And thousands of medical and health-care professionals are joining their ranks. They advocate total prohibitions on animal experimentation, or they look for ways to limit it. They say animal research isn't really applicable to humans and diverts money from more useful clinical research.

Many medical researchers, however, argue that animals are crucial to research. Dr. Fred Epstein, director of New York University Medical Center's division of Pediatric Neurosurgery, used cats to develop new surgical treatments in the early 1970s for children with excess fluid on the brain.

He says he used the technique to save the lives of 20 children, and that it improved the quality of life for thousands of others. "This is black and white," says Epstein. "It's not debatable. These children are alive because of what we learned."

Animal Rights Poll

For both statements, mark whether you agree, feel neutral, disagree or aren't sure. Then compare your answers with the results of a poll of more than 500 people.

	Agree	Neutral	Disagree	Not Sure
1. It should be against the law to use animals such as dogs, cats and monkeys for medical experimentation.				
2. New medicine should be tested on animals before it's tried on humans.				

Actual Polled Responses:	Agree	Neutral	Disagree	Not Sure
For statement #1	32%	4%	58%	6%
For statement #2	49%	4%	42%	5%

Discussion Starters

● Should scientists experiment on animals to gather medical information they can use with humans? Why or why not? If you had a terminal disease that doctors might find a cure for through animal experimentation, how would you feel about those experiments?

● Read Matthew 10:29-31 and 12:11-12. How does God compare humans with animals? Is it okay to hurt an animal to help a human? Why or why not? Is God concerned when an animal suffers? Why or why not?

● Read Genesis 1:24-30 and Genesis 9:3. What is humanity's responsibility toward animals? If it's cruel to experiment on animals, is it cruel to eat animals too? Why or why not? According to these passages what are the differences between animals and humans? Do animals have eternal souls? Why or why not? Read Deuteronomy 14:2-21. Is it okay to experiment on or eat some animals but not others? Explain.

● Read 1 Corinthians 13:1-10 and Colossians 3:12. Is it possible to love an animal the same way you love a human? Why or why not? Is it love if you sacrifice an animal's life to help save a human's life? Explain. How do these scripture guidelines apply to our relationships with animals?

● Do the "Animal Rights Poll." How did your answers compare with the results of the poll?

● Read Proverbs 10:14. Is it wise for us to "store up knowledge" about human medical problems? Why or why not? What are other ways we can cure diseases without harming animals?

Motorists Keep Money Found on Interstate

COLUMBUS, Ohio—An armored truck's rear door swung open on Interstate 71 and sent bills from 10s to 100s flying. The truck continued for at least a mile before the driver realized what had happened.

People driving on the freeway picked up the cash. And witnesses said one woman stuffed cash into her underclothes. The Dispatch, the city's daily newspaper, quoted sources as saying more than $1 million was lost.

But not everyone kept the cash. Melvin Kaiser, an Ohio Bell phone technician, turned over $57,000 he recovered on the freeway. Kaiser said he considered keeping the money, but couldn't keep it in good conscience. Kaiser was then rewarded with a check equal to 10 percent of the amount he turned in.

The incident created an ethical debate throughout the city. At radio station WNCI, phone calls jammed the switchboard when announcers reported the spill. More than 90 percent of the callers said they would've kept the cash.

Finders Keepers

What things would you keep if you found them? Circle the items below that you would definitely keep. Put a question mark over the ones you're unsure whether you'd keep, and mark an "X" over the items you definitely wouldn't keep.

Discussion Starters

● What would you think if you saw thousands of dollars on the freeway? What would you do? Why did so many people keep the money they found? Why did Melvin Kaiser turn in the money he found? Were the people who kept the money right or wrong? Explain.

● Did Kaiser get a fair reward? Why or why not? Would you turn in the money if you knew there was no reward? Why or why not?

● Read Isaiah 33:15-16 and 2 Corinthians 13:7. What should Christians do if they find something that's not theirs? If you don't know who owns the item, what should you do?

● Read 2 Corinthians 8:21. What example did Kaiser set? Was he foolish or smart to give the money back? Explain. Read 1 Thessalonians 4:11-12. What does it mean to mind your own business? Would you act differently knowing God's watching you? Why or why not?

● Do the "Finders Keepers" box. Then discuss it with a friend.

● Read Genesis 43:1-28. How does this story apply to the people who found the money? Is it wrong to keep something you find? Why or why not?

NASA Plans to Spend Billions on Exploration

WASHINGTON—The National Aeronautics and Space Administration (NASA) has an ambitious space exploration program that could establish a manned lunar observatory, put astronauts on the Martian moon Phobos or send them to the red planet itself by early in the 21st century. The plan will probably cost close to $25 billion a year, or 4 percent of the U.S. budget.

NASA's plan was unveiled in the report "Beyond Earth's Boundaries: Human Exploration of the Solar System in the 21st Century." The report is in response to a presidential directive "to expand human presence and activity beyond Earth orbit into the solar system."

The report focuses on four space exploration case studies. One would send astronauts to Phobos and then on to Mars. Another would launch astronauts directly to Mars. A third would establish a manned observatory on the moon. A fourth would use an outpost on the moon as a steppingstone to Mars.

John Aaron, who served as assistant administrator of exploration during the production of the report, says the agency did not have specific cost estimates for the missions. "We are not talking about missions that are cheap," he said, adding: "We think these are affordable."

Frank Martin, Aaron's successor, said: "You can't do the civil space program on the cheap. We're not a poor nation. We can figure out how to do these things if they're important to us."

Discussion Starters

● Should the United States spend close to $25 billion annually on space exploration? Why or why not? Should we spend any money at all on space exploration? Why or why not? What benefits could we reap by sending astronauts to Mars? Do you think God created life elsewhere in the universe? Explain.

● Read Psalm 19:1. Can we learn about God from space exploration? Why or why not? What's the relationship between heaven and space?

● Read Matthew 17:19-20. What are officials at NASA putting their faith in when they make plans to put a person on Mars? Is nothing impossible for us when we put our faith in technology? Why or why not?

● Read 1 Corinthians 8:1-3. Does our knowledge of other planets—and our ability to send people to study them—make us arrogant? Why or why not?

● Read Matthew 23:23. Do you think we spend too much time and money on relatively unimportant things while neglecting things such as justice and mercy for one another? Why or why not? Read Galatians 6:10 and James 1:27. Since we have limited resources, which of our society's primary needs should we spend our money on? Does space exploration help us "do good to all people"? Why or why not?

● Read Matthew 25:31-46. If we spend money on space exploration, does that make us better sheep or better goats? Explain. Do you think we'll find knowledge through space exploration that will help the poor and needy? Why or why not?

Discussion Starters

• Should the United States spend close to $27 billion annually on space exploration? Why or why not? Should we spend any money at all on space exploration? Why or why not? What benefits could we reap by sending astronauts to Mars? Does or didn't God created life elsewhere in the universe? Explain.

• Read Psalm 19:1. What we can learn about God from space exploration? Why or why not? What is the relation/trip between heaven and space?

• Read Matthew 6:19-20. What are effects on NASA putting their faith in when they mine plans to put a portion on Earth? Is it more important to focus when we put event faith in technology? Why or why not?

• Read 1 Corinthians 8:1,3. Does our knowledge of other planets— and our ability to send people to study them—make us arrogant? Why or why not?

• Read Matthew 25:23. Do you think we spend too much time and money on relatively unimportant things while neglecting things such as justice and mercy for one another? Why or why not? Read Galatians 6:10 and James 1:27. Since we have limited resources, which of our society's primary focus should we spend our money on? Does space exploration help us do good to all people? Why or why not?

• Read Matthew 25:31-46. If we spend money on space exploration, does that make us help others or better space? Explain. Do you think we'll find it easy enough through space exploration that will help the poor and needy? Why or why not?

SECTION TWO:
Religion

Woman Refuses to Work on Sabbath; Gets Fired

ALTAMONTE SPRINGS, Fla.— After working for her employer for more than two years, a woman was fired after she became a Seventh-day Adventist and refused to work on Saturday, her church's Sabbath.

At first there was no problem: Paula Hobbie's supervisor at Lawton and Company, a Florida jewelry store, adjusted the work schedule. For two months, the supervisor worked Friday evenings and Saturdays, and Hobbie worked Sundays.

But then upper management told Hobbie she had to work on Saturdays or else quit. When she refused to do either, she was fired.

Risky Business

Which church activities would you insist on attending, even if it meant risking losing your job? Rank them in order (1=you'd most likely risk your job; 5=you'd least likely risk your job).

- Weekly worship   _____
- Youth group meeting   _____
- Midweek Bible study   _____
- Weekend retreat   _____
- Weeklong youth group trip _____

Discussion Starters

● Was Paula Hobbie's employer justified in firing her? Why or why not?

● Should Hobbie have agreed to work on her Sabbath? Do you think she was using the Sabbath as an excuse to not work, or was her motive really worship? Explain.

● What if all people refused to work on their Sabbath days—Saturday for some, Sunday for others? Should you refuse to do homework on the Sabbath? Why or why not?

● Read Exodus 20:8-11. Who does God command not to work on the Sabbath? Read Exodus 31:12-17. What's the reason for not working on the Sabbath? Read verses 13 and 17. Is that reason still valid today? Explain.

● Read Colossians 2:16. How does this affect the Old Testament guidelines for the Sabbath?

● Read Colossians 3:16 and Hebrews 10:24-25. Does worship happen only with other people? Explain. If a Christian always worked on the Sabbath and couldn't meet with other Christians, would that affect his or her worship life? Why or why not?

● Read Hebrews 4:9-11. What is the connection between the "Sabbath-rest" and faith? Read John 4:21-24. Does this mean you don't need to go to a particular place—such as a church—to worship God?

● Read Matthew 6:19. How does earning money compare with spending time with God? What advice would you give someone who's struggling with working on the Sabbath?

● Do the "Risky Business" box. Discuss it with a friend.

Man Claims to Spend Five Days in Heaven

"Heaven is gold streaks and millions of kinds of instruments playing and singing to the glory of God ... There's no human mind can comprehend the beauty of heaven ... unless they've been there," says Rev. Dr. Percy Collett, 83.

Collett also says he's been there.

Collett was working as a medical missionary in the jungles of the Amazon River when, he says, he was called by an angel to visit heaven.

Heaven, according to Collett, is a planet 80 times bigger than Earth. Outer heaven is filled with trees and animals, he says, and people walk on gold and there are flowers and animals of all kinds. All of God's creatures except the snake live there and are praising God, Collett explains.

In heaven, claims Collett, are "thousands of souls," some of whom he recognized: John F. Kennedy; the Apostle Paul; thousands of martyrs; Abraham; Mary, the mother of Jesus; and Collett's own mother.

Collett's tour of heaven took five-and-a-half Earth days, he said. Before he left, "Jesus sat my soul down and ordained me." Collett says he returned to Earth with two charges: to share the reality of heaven with people on Earth and to tell of the "explosion of God's power" that is about to happen.

According to Collett, just before men attempt to start a nuclear war, God will intervene. Earth will "shake and rock and reel ... God is going to destroy all the creation of man," says Collett.

Heaven Is ...

What do you think heaven is like? Circle one answer in each phrase below.

Heaven is ...
- a relationship or a place.
- the reason for being a Christian or a bonus for Christians.
- like Earth, only better or like nothing we've ever seen.
- an end or endless.

Discussion Starters

● How do you feel about Collett's story?

● Would you have believed people in New Testament times when they told of Jesus' miracles? If so, shouldn't you believe Collett's story? If not, why not?

● Describe your reaction to each of Collett's statements:
1. There are "thousands of souls" ... including his own mother.
2. "Jesus sat my soul down and ordained me."
3. All of God's creatures except the snake live there and are praising God.
4. Just before men attempt to start a nuclear war, God will intervene.

● Read 1 Corinthians 2:6-16. How do Collett's story and Paul's writing compare? Read verse 9. How can Collett say he saw what no one has seen or understood? Why did God give him a "special" privilege? Read verse 10. Does God's Spirit tell everyone God's secrets—or only a few select people? Explain. Is heaven one of God's secrets? Why or why not?

● Read the following "heavenly" verses. Compare God's revelation to Collett's story and what you've always thought about heaven:
1 Corinthians 15:42-44; Philippians 3:21; Colossians 3:4; 1 Peter 5:10; 1 John 3:2; Revelation 7:16-17; and 21:4.

● Do the "Heaven Is ..." box. Compare your answers with a friend's.

Minor Evangelist's Tour Makes Major Money

ATLANTA—Evangelist Jim Whittington crisscrosses the country in his $350,000 custom motor home and holds outdoor revivals under a $42,000 red carnival tent. At a recent revival, Whittington interrupted his sermon on the evils of a nearby flea market to offer his listeners a deal. The first 40 people to give him a $100 donation would receive a special blessing and a shred of his handkerchief. "Only 40 can get in on this," he said. "Not 41." Prompted by an initial "gift" by one of Whittington's employees, 39 people quickly moved forward to buy out the rest of the "blessing."

Whittington says an average revival brings in $30,000. But his 500,000-name mailing list is even more lucrative. The return rate on his letters requesting donations is almost 12 percent, four times the average. What's his secret? A typical Whittington fund-raising letter offers a clue: "My Dear Friend ... Two of the people that raised their hand against my ministry are dead and the third one has a chronic lung disease ... I'm writing you because I believe you love this ministry. Don't you?"

With money generated from his revivals, Whittington paid cash for a big house near his Fountain of Life headquarters in Greenville, North Carolina. His Rolls-Royce, Cadillac and Lincoln are paid for. He wears two diamonds of more than six carats each, one he says was owned by Liberace. He bought his custom motor home after he saw a rock group riding in one. "Why criticize me over a few diamonds when the streets of heaven are paved with gold?" he asks.

Discussion Starters

● Read Luke 9:49-50. If Whittington tells people about salvation, but uses questionable means to do it, is he for or against God? Explain. If Whittington is against God, why does his ministry attract so many people? If he's for God, is it right to question his honesty or motives? Why or why not?

● Read Jeremiah 5:26-31. Is it right for Whittington to buy expensive cars and jewelry with money from his revivals? Why or why not?

● Read Jeremiah 5:31 again. God asks you a question at the end of this verse. What should you do about prophets who "prophesy lies"?

● Read 1 Corinthians 9:9-11. Should evangelists receive a salary for their work, or should they depend on donations? Explain. Should there be a limit to how much an evangelist can make? Why or why not?

● Read Revelation 21:10, 21. Whittington justified his diamond jewelry by saying "the streets of heaven are paved with gold." How do you feel about this statement?

● Read Matthew 19:21-26. If Whittington had been preaching when Jesus walked the Earth, what might Jesus have said to him? Is it possible to be rich and a Christian? Why or why not? How should you live out your Christian faith if you're rich? poor?

Woman Says Prayer Helped Her Win Lottery

As far as Regina Hammond is concerned, luck has little to do with it. The 37-year-old flight attendant won $100,000 in a Colorado lottery game, on top of $50,000 she won the previous year the same way. And she's not finished yet. Her goal is the $1 million grand prize.

Hammond believes prayer has paved her way to riches. "I pray to God to help me and he answers," she says.

Prayer Possibilities

Checkmark the items you'd feel comfortable praying for. Give reasons for your answers.

I'd pray for ...
- an A on a test._____
- lots of money._____
- getting a job._____
- a better complexion._____
- winning a game._____
- new clothes._____
- not getting caught drinking._____
- getting a date._____
- losing or gaining weight._____

Discussion Starters

● How does Regina Hammond's claim make you feel? If prayer works, why don't all lottery players pray and win? Do you think Hammond will win the million dollars? Why or why not?

● Should people pray to get rich? to win sports events? to be successful? Explain.

● Some people feel lotteries are illegal and sinful. If that's true, why would God answer Hammond's prayers to win? Would you pray to win a lottery? Why or why not?

● Read Matthew 7:7-8 and 21:22. If this is true, why don't all people who pray receive what they want? What if two Christians pray for opposite things; do the prayers cancel out each other? Why or why not?

● Read Psalm 19:14; Mark 11:4; and Philippians 4:6. Does God answer all prayers? Explain. If we don't pray "correctly," does that mean God won't answer our prayers? Explain. Read James 1:6-8. How does God answer prayers?

● Read Isaiah 65:24. If God already knows what we're going to pray for, why is it necessary to pray?

● Read Matthew 8:2; Luke 22:42; and 1 John 5:14. How do we know what God's will is when we pray? Is it necessary to always say "if it's God's will"? Why or why not?

● What prayers have you prayed and then been disappointed in God's answers? What have you prayed and then been glad for God's answers?

● Read 2 Corinthians 12:8-10. How can God's grace be sufficient, even when you wish things were different?

● Do the "Prayer Possibilities" box. Discuss it with a friend.

Church Member Shares Beer With Teenagers

David Banovich, member of the Alpha and Omega Church, drank beer with two teenagers on the way to youth camp. "I just felt that the Holy Spirit was leading me into doing it with them, to break down the barriers," he says. "I didn't raise a big deal about it."

In fact, neither did the mother of one of the teenagers. She told Banovich she'd rather have her son drinking beer with an adult than out driving and getting "bombed out of his mind."

Banovich, a volunteer high school counselor, says what he did was okay. "I believe that Christian churches, Christianity, will kill more young people than alcohol and drugs will this year," he says. Banovich believes the church's rules and regulations force many teenagers into using alcohol and drugs and having sex.

Discussion Starters

● Do you approve of what David Banovich did? Why or why not?

● Do you agree or disagree with the mother who said she'd rather have her son drinking beer with an adult than out driving and getting "bombed out of his mind"? Would the teenagers have gotten "bombed out of their minds" if they hadn't had a beer with the church member? Why or why not?

● Explain why you agree or disagree with: "I believe that Christian churches, Christianity, will kill more young people than alcohol and drugs will this year."

● Do rules help or hinder a person's growth? Explain. Read Matthew 5:17-18. When Jesus says he didn't come to do away with the law, does that mean we still live under Old Testament rules? Why or why not?

● Read Matthew 7:1. Could this verse be used to support Banovich's actions? Why or why not?

● Read Proverbs 20:1 and Mark 2:16-17. How are the two messages similar? different?

● It's illegal for teenagers to drink beer in almost every state. According to Banovich, the Holy Spirit led him to drink with the kids. Do you think the Holy Spirit would ever lead someone to do something illegal? Why or why not?

● Read Hebrews 13:17. What does this verse say about following spiritual leaders? If your youth leader suggested drinking beer with the group, what would you do? Would you tell your parents or other youth leaders? Why or why not?

Woman Faces Jail for Taking Kids to Church

DENVER—A Catholic woman faces a jail sentence for contempt of court after she violated a Denver court order requiring her to raise her two children as Jews.

In an unusual divorce ruling, district judge Leslie Lawson granted 36-year-old Dorothy Boeke's ex-husband, a Jew, "religious custody." Even though the mother remarried and joined the Catholic Church, she was not allowed to take Rachel, 7, and Lauren, 5, to regular church services. She did anyway, and now her ex-husband wants the court to intervene.

"This is the first time this has happened in Colorado and the fourth time in the United States," says Boeke. "It's really an unusual circumstance." District judge Connie Peterson says: "It is uncommon. Religion is mostly determined by the parent who has custody."

Boeke converted to Judaism 11 years ago, shortly before she married Jerold Simms, now her ex-husband. She says the decision was made "when I was young and foolish ... I should have listened to my mother. Mixed marriages just don't work."

The couple raised their two children as Jews until they separated. Boeke then rejoined the Catholic Church and began attending daily Mass. She contends she has obeyed the court order by sending her children to Hebrew school on Saturdays.

"Nowhere in the court order does it say I cannot take them to church," says Boeke. "I go to daily Mass and I'm not going to get a babysitter. They don't receive communion, they simply go along like we go to Safeway [a grocery store]."

In court documents, Simms agreed to let the children attend Mass on Easter and Christmas, but he claims the girls "are suffering substantial emotional harm and confusion" from the frequent churchgoing.

Discussion Starters

● Which parent should determine the religious upbringing of the two girls? Explain. Read Hebrews 13:17 and 1 Peter 2:13-15. Was it a sin for Boeke to defy the court ruling and take her daughters to church? Why or why not? Does the court have a right to dictate the religion Boeke chooses to raise her children in? Why or why not?

● Read Acts 5:17-29. If you were Boeke, would you go to jail rather than stop your children from going to church with you? Explain. How do you know when it's right in God's eyes to disobey an authority? If an authority such as the court makes an unjust decision, how are we supposed to respond as Christians? Do you think Rachel and Lauren will suffer "substantial emotional harm and confusion" from practicing both faiths? Why or why not?

● Read Hebrews 10:23-25. How important is it for Rachel and Lauren to attend Mass regularly? Should the two children have the right to decide which church to attend? Why or why not? If the kids aren't allowed to attend Mass, how will that affect their relationship with their mother?

● Read Proverbs 22:6. Who has the ultimate right to "train a child in the way he should go": the father, mother or government? Explain.

● Read Ephesians 6:1-4 and Colossians 3:20-21. How can kids follow the command to "obey your parents" when their parents are divorced? What's the best way for Rachel and Lauren to honor both parents? to honor God? Are both parents trying to follow the command in Ephesians 6:4? Why or why not?

● Read 2 Corinthians 6:14. How important is it to marry another Christian? Would you marry someone of another Christian denomination? a Jew? an atheist? Why or why not?

Woman Dies From Fast

GRAND MARAIS, Minn.—Dawn Marie Purchase, 21, died from dehydration. The county chief deputy says she went 13 days without food or water at a campsite in the Boundary Waters Canoe Area (BWCA).

Purchase and her boyfriend, Rick Saver, went to the BWCA to find themselves and see what they could do with their lives.

"They were taking the summer to canoe, study the Bible, get to know God better and achieve spiritual awareness," says Chief Deputy Dick Dorr. "Part of their experience eventually included this fast."

A University of Minnesota expert on starvation says the body can go a lot longer than 13 days without food. But the body needs water. He believes 13 days with no water or food most likely caused Purchase's death.

Getting Closer to God

Read 2 Peter 1:3-11. Peter talks about seven qualities that can make you more like God. On the chart below, write the qualities you have and those you need to work on in the appropriate columns. Then list specific ways you can grow in the areas needing improvement.

Qualities I Have	Qualities to Work On	What I Can Do to Improve

Discussion Starters

● How do you feel about Dawn and Rick's method of getting closer to God? Why did they fast? Why did Dawn fast so long?

● Did Dawn and Rick choose positive ways to get to know God better? Why or why not?

● Read Joel 2:12-17. Why did the people fast? How important was this fast? Read Luke 4:1-13. How long did Jesus fast? If Jesus could fast that long, why can't we?

● Look at Isaiah 58:1-12 and Zechariah 7:1-6. Do people always fast for good reasons? Why or why not? How could Dawn's fast have been a poor idea? a good one?

● Read Matthew 6:16-18. What guidelines exist for fasting? Why is it important no one knows you're fasting?

● Read Psalm 119:1-8 and 1 Peter 2:1-10. How can you grow closer to God? Does that include fasting? Why or why not?

● During Lent (40 days before Easter), people often give up something or fast. Why? Have you ever tried fasting? If so, when? How did you feel? What happened to your relationship with God during that time? If you haven't ever fasted, why haven't you?

● Do the "Getting Closer to God" box. In what ways can you become closer to God? Choose one to concentrate on this week.

SECTION THREE:
School

Student Test Canceled After Answers Published

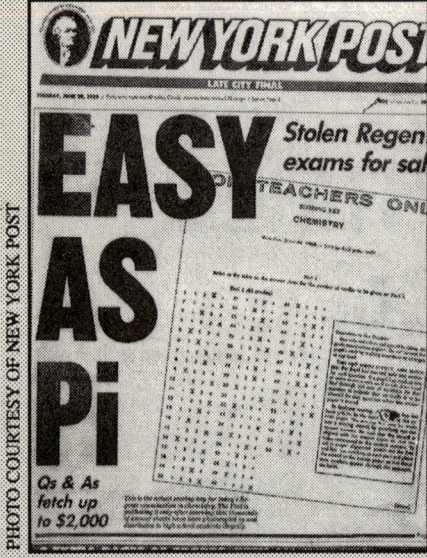

PHOTO COURTESY OF NEW YORK POST

ALBANY, N.Y.—A statewide high school achievement test was canceled after the New York Post published the answers to the chemistry exam on its front page to demonstrate what it called a growing black market in stolen exams. About 80,000 students statewide take the exam.

State education commissioner Thomas Sobol called the Post "beneath contempt" and threatened to sue the newspaper. The cost of providing a new exam to students would be $250,000. Sobol said officials were investigating the theft of the chemistry test and others after learning the exams were "widely available" to students in New York City.

The tests, given in 17 subjects during the summer, are taken by college-bound high school students in New York state and generally account for about a quarter of a student's final grade.

Timothy Gilles of the state attorney general's office said his office was investigating reports that the tests and answers were being sold for $2,000, although some tests were available for as little as $5 or $10 the night before the exam.

Post editor Jerry Nachman said it took a reporter 15 minutes to find a copy of a test after he was assigned the story. "We did not contaminate a test by publishing a key," said Nachman. "We published a key that had been contaminated."

Discussion Starters

● Was the New York Post right to print the test answers on the front page? Why or why not? Should the state education commissioner sue the newspaper for printing the test answers? Why or why not? If you were state education commissioner, would you have canceled the test?

● Why are test answers so readily available? Who's guiltier: the people selling the answers or the people buying them? Explain.

● Read Proverbs 9:17. How do you feel after you've cheated on a test or lied? If someone offered you the answers to an important test, what would you do?

● Read Matthew 10:26-27 and Ephesians 5:11-13. If you found out test answer keys were widely available for a price, would you tell school officials? a newspaper reporter? your parents? your youth leader? your friends? Why or why not?

● Who do cheaters really hurt? What consequences do cheaters face for their cheating later in life? When—if ever—is cheating justified?

● Read 1 Corinthians 6:9-11 and 1 John 3:4-10. Is it okay to cheat as long as you're not hurting someone else? What's the difference between someone who "sins" and a person who "continues to sin"? What does it mean to "inherit the kingdom of God"? Did the New York Post do the "righteous" thing by printing the test answers? Why or why not?

● Read Matthew 5:29-30 and 15:10-20. To Jesus, why is cheating so bad? How could you live out Jesus' command to "gouge [your eye] out" when tempted to cheat?

Principal Has Teacher Change Athlete's Grade

JACKSBORO, Tenn.—The principal walked into Ann McGhee's classroom and told her he would watch her class while she stepped out to change an "F" to a "D minus" on a basketball player's grade report.

McGhee, who complied with the request, resigned at the end of the day.

"I don't feel that I would be effective as a teacher any longer because anything that I said for the students to do would be a joke," she said.

The student whose grade got changed was a star member of the school's undefeated basketball team.

Making the Grade

Think of difficult situations in your life. How do you stand up for your values and beliefs? For each situation below, write how you react and then "grade" your reaction. Use an A for God-pleasing reactions; a C for reactions made according to your feelings—sometimes right, sometimes wrong; and an F for reactions you know are wrong. Explain your answers.

Situation	How you react	Grade
When others start gossiping		
When there's a chance to copy someone's homework or test answers		
When someone makes fun of your beliefs		
When someone lies to you		
When someone doesn't like you		
When church seems boring		
When you get angry		
When you're teased		
When someone swears		

Discussion Starters

● What surprises you most about this situation?

● Should the teacher have resigned? Why or why not? What would justify the principal's request to change the grade?

● Should the failing star basketball player receive special privileges? Why or why not? What's more important: an undefeated basketball team or high academic standards? Explain. What's more important in your school?

● Do you agree that the teacher wouldn't be effective as a teacher since she changed the grade? Why or why not?

● Could the athlete's grade-change make the other students view their assignments as "a joke"? Why or why not? Would the teacher or the other students be more upset about the grade-change? Explain.

● Was it worth the teacher's job for her to stand up for her beliefs? Why or why not? Who had the strongest value statement in the situation? the principal? the teacher? the basketball player?

● Read Matthew 5:38-42; 18:21-22; and 1 Thessalonians 5:15. What do these words say about doing something even if you don't feel like it? When is it okay to stand up for what you believe is right?

● Read James 1:2-4. Does this mean the teacher should've stayed on the job and endured? Why or why not? When is it right to endure a situation and when is it okay to give up? What are the positive and negative aspects of "getting out" to prove a point?

● Read 1 Peter 2:15-17. What good did the teacher do? Who was the teacher respecting most by resigning? herself? the principal? the athlete? the other students? Explain.

● Do the "Making the Grade" box. What did you learn about yourself? Choose two C or F situations. Decide what practical steps you can take to improve your "grade."

Professor Requires Students to Risk Failure

ANN ARBOR, Mich.—"Failure 101" is visiting professor Jack Matson's school of hard knocks for University of Michigan students. Matson, who wears a combat helmet in class to show that the business world is a war zone, says most students are so afraid of failure they won't take risks necessary for successful entrepreneurship.

Matson is a self-described failure: "My engineering design firm in Houston went belly-up a few years ago," he says. Naturally, students are required to risk failure in their entrepreneurial projects.

The course, officially called Innovative Entrepreneurship, has been a success for the university's school of business administration. Dean Gilbert Whitaker says, "Most business courses are so analytical and structured that it's refreshing when someone can liven and leaven one."

One semester, Matson started his 50 students with a project to create "something of value" out of Popsicle sticks. Students had to each give a marketing pitch for their product to classmates, who were encouraged by Matson to boo if they disapproved. Next, students were required to each sell their product on the streets. Products included a kite capable of flying only in gale-force winds and a hot tub for hamsters.

Some students did sell their products to passers-by for a dollar or two. "But," Matson says, "I told them: 'You blew it. You charged too little.'" If the products were easy to sell, he says, students should have risked raising prices.

Matson says students won't really learn anything unless they risk losing some of their own money. "It's the only way to learn innovation and get out of the play-it-safe rut that has put us behind the Japanese," he adds.

Are You a Failure?

For each area of your life, indicate where you're between success and failure by marking a dot at that point on the continuum.

Grades	Success ⊢————————⊣	Failure
Attitudes	Success ⊢————————⊣	Failure
Friends	Success ⊢————————⊣	Failure
Parents	Success ⊢————————⊣	Failure
Siblings	Success ⊢————————⊣	Failure
God	Success ⊢————————⊣	Failure
Dating	Success ⊢————————⊣	Failure
Sports	Success ⊢————————⊣	Failure

Discussion Starters

● Would you enjoy learning from a teacher who required you to experience failure? Why or why not? Is it right to think of the business world as a war zone? Why or why not?

● Read Matthew 17:15-20 and Mark 9:24-29. Do you think the disciples' faith grew or decreased because of their failures? Explain. Describe a time when you failed because you had "so little faith." What did you learn from the experience? If you could live your life over again, would you avoid or relive the failures you've experienced so far?

● Read Genesis 11:3-8 and Numbers 14:40-45. Is it possible to succeed in life if you're not doing what God wants you to do? Why or why not? Why are the consequences of failure so harsh sometimes? What would happen to us if the negative consequences of failure were taken away?

● Read Luke 14:28-33. What's the difference between making a foolish decision and making a good, but risky decision? What does it mean to "estimate the cost" in your relationship with God? Is it risky to trust your life to God? Explain.

● Read Matthew 14:22-33. Who experienced the bigger failure: Peter or the disciples in the boat? Explain. Exactly why did Peter fail? How have you failed in a similar way? Is failure necessary for personal growth? Why or why not?

● Read Matthew 10:38-39 and 19:16-26. Why does Jesus say we must give up what's most important to us to find life? What does "losing your life" mean to you? Is there anything in your life you'd be unwilling to give over to God? Why or why not?

● Read Matthew 27:33-46. Was Jesus' earthly life a failure? Why or why not? Do the "Are You a Failure" box. Read Romans 8:35-39. No matter whether you see yourself more as a success or failure, God loves you and wants to be with you forever.

Teacher Expects Too Much of His Students

CHARLESTON, W.Va.—A principal evaluated Larry Brown and said the eighth-grade science teacher needs to change his expectations of students. The Blennerhassett Junior High School principal claimed that Brown failed to monitor his students' progress and gave too many D's and F's.

During the first two quarters of school, Brown gave half his students D's or F's. He said most students scored poorly on tests, and few finished their assignments. Brown said on one assignment only four of 18 students turned in their papers. Of those four, only one was complete.

High Expectations

How much do people expect from you? For each person or category of people, place an X in the appropriate column.

Who	Expectations			
	Too much	The right amount	Too little	Doesn't apply
Parents				
Teachers				
Youth leader				
Myself				
Siblings				
Friends				
Employer				
Coaches				
Pastor				

Discussion Starters

● Why did the principal say the teacher needs to change his expectations? Do you agree with the principal? Why or why not?

● Was Larry Brown fair to his students or did he grade them too hard? Explain.

● Should students fail when they don't turn in assignments? Why or why not? If a student fails, is it the teacher's fault, the student's fault or both? Explain.

● Was the teacher wrong to grade so hard? Why or why not?

● Read Matthew 5:48. What kind of expectation does God have of you? What does it mean to be perfect in Christ? Explain.

● Read Deuteronomy 32:4. Discuss God's attributes that Moses describes. How can you put on these attributes too?

● Read James 3:1-2. Did the principal grade the teacher too hard? Why or why not?

● Read Ecclesiastes 12:12. Do you think the students didn't turn in their assignments because the teacher demanded too much of them? If so, why? If not, why did the students do poorly on their tests and not turn in their assignments?

● Read 1 Chronicles 28:10-21. Did God expect too much of Solomon? Why or why not? Do you work harder when more is expected of you or when less is expected? Explain.

● Read 2 Corinthians 13:5-11. Does this passage apply to the teacher's grading? Why or why not? How does it apply to the principal's evaluation? How do these words apply to you and your performance?

● Do the "High Expectations" box. How do you react to high expectations? Are there limits to expectations? If so, what are they? If not, why not?

● How have others failed you when you expected a lot from them? Are high expectations good? Why or why not? Name three high expectations you have of yourself. What are you doing to meet them?

High School Yearbook Publishes Racial Slur

TAUNTON, Mass.—Taunton High School's yearbook published a racial slur, driving a white senior to tears. "Nigger lover," which appeared in 420 yearbooks, turned up under Carol Buczek's picture.

"I'm well-known at school," the 17-year-old said. "People could've called me anything if they had something against me, but to call me a 'nigger lover,' they knew it would get to my heart."

Buczek said the remark was published because of her best friend Donna Houston. Buczek and Houston have been friends since sixth grade.

The racial slur appeared under Buczek's name in the section where each student wrote his or her autobiography. The statement turned up at the end of the subsection titled "Memories."

Although the school has a 4 percent minority enrollment, headmaster Peter P. George said he never encountered racial problems before. "We have one person who is sick, who has a warped mind and who thought it would be a big joke to use that term under that lady's name," George said. "I am convinced there is no racism in this school or in this community."

Discussion Starters

● Why did students publish the racial slur in the high school yearbook? Explain your answer. Do you agree with the headmaster that no racism exists in his school or community? Why or why not?

● Why didn't the students publish a racial slur under Donna Houston's picture? If they would have, what would they have written? How do you feel about the person who wrote the statement? Why did the statement upset Carol Buczek?

● Read Proverbs 26:18-19. How might this apply to the student who wrote the statement? When is a joke harmful? How have you felt when you've been the victim of a joke?

● Read 1 Corinthians 4:10-13. Was Buczek persecuted? Why or why not? How should she react to the incident? Read John 15:11-13. Should you get hurt in order to keep a friend? Why or why not? How much should you let others hurt you?

● Compare Exodus 21:22-25 with Matthew 6:14-15. According to these passages, how should Buczek treat the person who wrote "nigger lover" under her name? In which passage is the punishment more fair?

● Discuss a time when others hurt you. How did it feel? When you're teased, do you accept it and believe it's part of being a Christian? Why or why not?

● What jokes have you played on people? Were any taken the wrong way? Why do some people not take humor well? What will you do in the future if someone plays a harmful joke on someone else? What is your responsibility as a Christian?

Teenager Says Her Figure Nixed Her Cheerleading

SANTA ANA, Calif.—People often joke about large breasts. But it was no laughing matter when a California high school senior was told she didn't make the cheerleading squad because her breasts were too large.

Vicki Ann Guest, 17, filed a $1 million lawsuit against her school district after a teacher allegedly told the teenager her grades and performance were acceptable, but her figure wasn't.

"What upset me was that my daughter believed this," Vicki's mother said at a news conference. "She thought her body was wrong. She was embarrassed. She just wanted to die."

The school principal said Vicki's skills were what kept her from making the squad—not her physical appearance.

Body Stereotypes

Write what abilities you associate with each of the following body types. Tell why.

Discussion Starters

● How would you feel if you were Vicki? her mother? her teacher? her school principal?

● Should Vicki have made the cheerleading squad? Why or why not? Why did she file a lawsuit? What if she really wasn't skilled enough?

● Do you need certain physical characteristics to be a cheerleader? Why or why not? What other activities require certain "bodies"; for example, football, gymnastics or ballet? Is it bad that some activities work best if a person has a certain physique? Can any "body" do any sport or activity? Explain. Should people be restricted from certain activities because of their physical appearance? Why or why not?

● Read 1 Samuel 16:7 and Galatians 2:6. What do these verses say about judging appearances? How do they apply to Vicki? to how you view your school's cheerleaders? to your view of your body? What's most important to God?

● Read 1 Corinthians 3:16-17 and 6:19-20. If God doesn't judge by appearances, why does he call our bodies "temples"? Does it matter how people look if their bodies are temples for the Holy Spirit? Explain.

● Read Luke 12:22-23 and Ephesians 5:29. What do these verses say about your body's importance? How do most people feel about their bodies? Does that attitude reflect God's idea about our bodies? Why or why not? Who or what most influences your body image?

● How would you help Vicki feel better about herself if you were her best friend?

● What can you do to feel better about your body?

● Do the "Body Stereotypes" box. Is it wrong to stereotype bodies and abilities? Why or why not?

Black Principal Faces Problems and Prejudice

FAIRVIEW, Tenn.—Students of this virtually all-white town have harassed the black high school principal with pranks such as setting off fire alarms, walking out of classes and staying home from school.

Freeman Cooper, 56, received his job as principal through a federal court order. The ruling was the result of a racial discrimination suit Cooper lodged against Williamson County after being passed over for a promotion.

Cooper arrives at work with the school board's blessing and occasionally a police escort. Each day he faces the apparent hatred of the 500 students—all except one are white.

But Cooper is taking it in stride. "I'm not really tense," he says. "I know how to forgive."

The students, however, aren't as content. Once they staged an afternoon walkout. Following the walkout the school superintendent lodged charges of incompetence and insubordination against Cooper and asked the school board to fire him. After a hearing, the school board voted to dismiss the charges against Cooper.

The students, according to classmate Tamara Jordan, are upset because during the hearing Cooper called five teachers who testified against him liars.

"It's bad the school has come to this," Jordan says.

Discussion Starters

● What's the reason for all the trouble? Who's at fault—Freeman Cooper, the federal court, the school board, the students? Explain.

● Why would Cooper fight to get a job there? What is he proving? Should people "fight" to be hired like Cooper did? Why or why not? What do people learn from racial discrimination?

● How would the situation be better or worse if Cooper left? If you were Cooper would you stay? Why or why not?

● Is Cooper being persecuted for his beliefs? Explain. Read Luke 6:22-23 and 2 Corinthians 6:3-10. Does persecution for beliefs make someone happy? Why or why not?

● If you were one of the white Fairview High students, how would you feel about a black principal? How would the situation be different if Cooper were white? Is prejudice ever good? Why or why not? Why are people prejudiced?

● Read Luke 6:37. What do judging and forgiving have to do with prejudice? Do Cooper's words "I know how to forgive" and calling five teachers liars contradict? Why or why not? What is forgiveness?

● Read Galatians 3:26-28 and Ephesians 2:11-18. What keeps people from being "one in Christ" and seeing each other as equals? Can a Christian be prejudiced? Why or why not?

● Read John 4:1-29. What can be learned about prejudice from this story? If Jesus went to Fairview High School, what would he tell the people there? If you could give advice to Cooper, what would you say? What would you say to the students?

Teenage Tycoons Find Success in Business

NEW YORK—A growing number of schools across the United States are teaching students to start and operate real businesses. Many of the programs—designed to create jobs for high schoolers—generate thousands of dollars of income. And students get caught up in making money.

"I want enough money to go anywhere, any time, at a moment's notice by any means," said one 18-year-old student.

Some educators worry that such classes will cause young people to become too materialistic. According to Joanne Ciulla, a business-ethics teacher at Wharton College, teenage entrepreneurs who believe money can make their dreams come true aren't willing to think about much besides their careers.

"We've reached a point in our culture where work is the sole source of happiness," she said.

Money, Money, Money

Look up each Bible passage, then fill in the information in each column.

Bible passage	Situation	What it says about riches or money (material possessions)	How you can apply this to your view of money
Genesis 39:2-5			
Joshua 6:15-19			
1 Kings 3:9-13			
2 Kings 12:4-5			
Matthew 6:24-34			
Matthew 19:16-24			
Matthew 25:1-30			
Mark 14:3-9			
Mark 14:10-11			

Discussion Starters

● Should schools offer courses in making money? Why or why not? How interested would you be in enrolling in a course that taught money-making? Explain. What's good about teenagers learning to make money? What's not so good?

● How would you respond to the student who said, "I want enough money to go anywhere, any time, at a moment's notice by any means"?

● How might teaching kids to start and operate businesses teach them to be materialistic? How do you feel about the statement: "work is the sole source of happiness"?

● If the programs create jobs for students, what's so bad about that? Explain. Do you agree that teenagers who believe money can make their dreams come true aren't willing to think about much besides their careers? Why or why not?

● Read Matthew 5:3-12. Does money have anything to do with happiness? Can having money help or hinder you in being a Christian?

● Read Acts 20:35b. Do you agree that if you had more money, you'd be able to give more money—and therefore be happier? Explain.

● Does a job ever conflict with church activities? Why or why not?

● Do the "Money, Money, Money" box. What's the greatest struggle you have concerning money? What's God's desire for you and money?

SECTION FOUR:
Sexuality

Abortion Pill Raises New Birth Control Questions

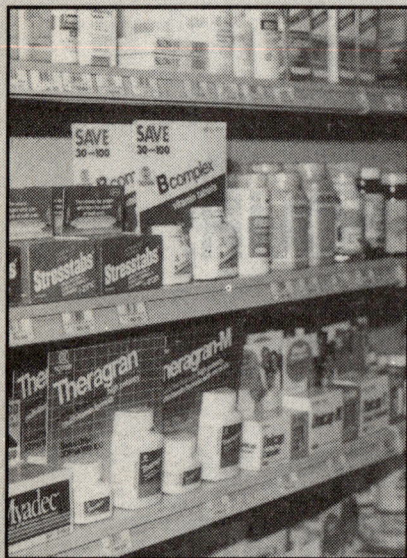

BOSTON—A pill that causes drug-induced abortions may be available in the United States sometime in the 1990s.

"Women have looked for a drug that will bring on a period when a period is late," said Dr. Allan Rosenfield of Columbia University. "This drug will do that. The woman doesn't need to know if she is pregnant."

Dr. William F. Crowley of Massachusetts General Hospital is troubled by the possibility that women might use the pill to induce abortions rather than practice regular birth control. "If this became a primary method of contraception for large numbers of people, it's a distressing thing," he said.

Many doctors look at the pill as an advantage over surgical abortions, which often cause complications. Others are concerned about the possible side effects the pill would have on the fetus if the pill didn't produce an abortion.

What's Worse?

Rank what you feel is the worse fate for the baby (1=the worst; 5=the best of the bad situations).

- being aborted by a pill _____
- growing up in an abusive home _____
- growing up on welfare _____
- being mentally or or physically handicapped _____
- being given up for adoption _____

Discussion Starters

● How do you feel about the abortion pill?

● Is it good or bad that the abortion pill is an easier abortion method than surgery? Explain. Is it a benefit that a woman "doesn't need to know if she is pregnant"? Why or why not?

● Why might women regularly use the abortion pill rather than birth control? How is the abortion pill like or unlike other forms of birth control?

● If the abortion pill is cheaper than surgical abortions, would abortions increase? Why or why not?

● If the abortion pill had always been available, how would history be different? What if Mary (Matthew 1:18) had taken an abortion pill because she wasn't married? Or Elizabeth (Luke 1:13, 18) or Sarah (Genesis 18:10-11) because they were older?

● What if your mom had taken an abortion pill or considered taking one when she was pregnant with you?

● If all the fetuses who've been aborted were born instead, what would the world be like?

● If God gave people the option to make choices ever since the Garden of Eden, is it okay to choose an abortion? Why or why not?

● Complete the "What's Worse?" box. Who should decide what's best for the baby? Why?

● Read Genesis 6:5-7. When a woman regrets getting pregnant and decides to have an abortion, how is that like God regretting making man and deciding to destroy him?

● Read Psalm 139:13-16. Did God know you before conception, immediately at conception or only after a certain point? How does that apply to abortion? Is God responsible for the birth of a baby—or are humans? How would your answer affect your view of the abortion pill?

● Do you want the abortion pill to be available, or would you fight to prevent its use? Explain. What would you say to a pregnant friend who was considering taking the abortion pill?

Christians Debate Teen Use of Birth Control

If current trends continue, 40 percent of today's 14-year-old girls will get pregnant before they turn 20.

Almost everyone agrees that these statistics show a serious crisis. But not everyone agrees on how to respond. In his research, Josh McDowell discovered that 60 percent of Christian teenagers have sex before marriage. So the Christian author and speaker began his "Why Wait?" campaign.

McDowell believes the Bible makes it clear people should wait until marriage to have sex. He believes premarital sex is the number one hindrance to spiritual growth in the United States.

Not everyone agrees that telling teenagers to say no will solve the problem. Some teenagers will continue to be sexually active, they say, so sexually active teenagers should use birth control.

In his book, *Handling Your Hormones* (Harvest House), Jim Burns says: "If you choose to do wrong, for goodness' sake, use birth control to prevent any more heartache than you might already be causing by your actions."

Burns doesn't advocate premarital sex. But he believes teenagers should protect themselves if they choose to be sexually active.

What Do You Think?

Read each statement below. Then for each, circle either SA (strongly agree), A (agree), U (unsure), D (disagree), or SD (strongly disagree).

Statement	Your Response
• Teenagers should never use birth control.	SA A U D SD
• Teenagers should decide what's best for themselves concerning birth control.	SA A U D SD
• Married adults should be able to use birth control.	SA A U D SD
• Sexually active teenagers can only be responsible by stopping their sexual activity.	SA A U D SD

Discussion Starters

● Why do many teenagers have premarital sex?

● How can premarital sex be the number one hindrance to spiritual growth?

● How successful are efforts such as Josh McDowell's "Why Wait?" campaign? Should teenagers use birth control? Why or why not? How do you feel about Jim Burns' statement? Explain.

● Read 1 Corinthians 6:15-20. How should you use your body to glorify God? How can teenagers avoid sexual immorality?

● Look at Romans 14:1-4. Why does Paul say not to argue about personal opinions? Is birth control a disputable matter? Why or why not?

● Read Colossians 1:10. How should you live in order to please God? Can you please God by using birth control and being sexually active? Why or why not?

● Read Psalm 139. When did God know you? Look at verses 13-16. Will using birth control interfere with God's plan? Why or why not?

● Since the Bible never directly mentions birth control, what can you base your decision about birth control on?

● If your friend takes the opposite view from yours on birth control, what should you do? How can you remain friends with someone you disagree with?

● If you think using birth control is okay, at what age should teenagers be able to use it? If you think *teenagers* shouldn't use birth control, what do you think about *married adults* using birth control?

● Do the "What Do You Think?" box. Talk about your responses. Are some responses easier to choose than others? Explain.

● What would you tell a friend who's sexually active? Should he or she use birth control? Why or why not?

School May Suspend Kids for Public Affection

WARE, Mass.—Public display of affection in Ware High School could carry a high price—a three-day suspension.

The new policy resulted from a complaint by a teacher who said she felt embarrassed when she walked down the hallways and saw students in passionate embraces.

The student handbook bans "inappropriate display of affection."

Principal Peter Thamel gave the high schoolers a definition of "appropriate display" on the first day of school.

"It's what you might do in front of your folks at 11 o'clock in the morning, not what you do at home in your rec room at midnight," Thamel explained.

Appropriate Displays

Grade these "hallway" displays of affection. Give appropriate affection an A and inappropriate affection an I:

Display of Affection	Grade
a peck on the cheek	
holding hands	
arms around each other	
a smooch on the lips	
gazing into each other's eyes	
hands in each other's back pockets	
a passionate kiss	
a pat on the back	
tickling	

Discussion Starters

● Do you agree with the principal's definition of appropriate display of affection? Explain.

● Do the "Appropriate Displays" box. Discuss it with a friend.

● If you were walking down the hall, what display of affection would embarrass you? your parents? your teachers? Jesus?

● Why do students need to show affection in the halls? Is a public display of affection for the two "lovers" or for others to see? Explain.

● Read Song of Songs 1:1-4 and 8:6. Were these words spoken in private or public? Explain. What does this say about displaying affection? Were you surprised to find this in the Bible? Why or why not?

● Read Paul's advice in Romans 16:16; 1 Corinthians 16:20; 2 Corinthians 13:12; and 1 Thessalonians 5:26. Define a "holy kiss." When does displaying affection change from appropriate to inappropriate? What is the purpose of affection?

● Read Psalm 33:13-15. How do you think God feels about what goes on in your school's hallways? Read Luke 7:44-47. People frowned on the woman's display of affection. Do you agree or disagree with them? Does Jesus' response surprise you? Why or why not?

● Read Ephesians 5:8-11. How can you live like a child of the light? How does a Christian appropriately show affection to a friend? a date?

Reverend Distributes Condoms in Church

WILLIAMSVILLE, N.Y.—Saying that condoms symbolize sexual responsibility, Rev. Carl Titchener distributed boxes of the birth-control devices to his congregation.

Titchener told the Unitarian Universalist Church of Amherst that there are only two ways to prevent the spread of AIDS—by abstinence and the use of condoms. He also criticized a Vatican newspaper report that said changes in certain types of sexual behavior—not the distribution of free condoms—are needed to battle the spread of AIDS.

A group of protesters gathered in front of the church. "What the reverend is saying does more damage than good," said Marilou Bebak, a spokesperson for the group. She said the distribution of condoms encourages sexual promiscuity. The protesters carried placards that said "Promotion of Condoms Procures the Wrath of God" and "Only Chastity Will Stop AIDS."

But inside the church, Titchener was praised for his actions. "He was giving knowledge—the greatest gift a person can give," said one congregation member. The people gave Titchener a standing ovation and several rounds of applause.

Agree or Disagree?

For each statement, check the appropriate box. Explain your answers.

	Agree	Disagree
• Condoms symbolize sexual responsibility.	☐	☐
• Only abstinence and the use of condoms will prevent the spread of AIDS.	☐	☐
• Pastors should distribute condoms.	☐	☐
• Distribution of condoms encourages sexual promiscuity.	☐	☐
• Promotion of condoms procures the wrath of God.	☐	☐
• Only chastity will stop AIDS.	☐	☐
• Knowledge is the greatest gift a person can give.	☐	☐

Discussion Starters

● Would you have given Titchener a standing ovation? Why or why not? How would you have felt if you were in that congregation when Titchener handed out condoms? What message would you have gotten?

● Was Titchener condoning homosexuality and promiscuity by handing out condoms? Why or why not?

● How likely is it that someone who wasn't sexually active would become sexually active because his or her pastor provided condoms? Explain.

● How do you feel about what Titchener did? Will his actions prevent some people from getting AIDS? from dying of AIDS? Why or why not?

● What is considered responsible sexual activity? Why do some people refuse to abstain? Read Genesis 2:21-25. If sexuality is a gift from God, is church the logical place to deal with issues of sexuality? Explain.

● Read Hebrews 13:17. Should you always accept and obey what your pastor says? Explain.

● Read 1 Corinthians 6:12-20. What does this passage say about sexual activity? What does verse 13 mean in your life? Explain. Read Ephesians 5:3-5. According to verse 3, should sexual immorality be mentioned in church? Why or why not?

● Read 1 Corinthians 5:9-13. Does this mean you shouldn't associate with Christian friends who are sexually immoral, but it's okay to be with non-Christian friends who are sexually immoral? Explain. What does this passage say about judging people who might be sexually immoral? Compare these verses to Matthew 7:1-5.

● Do the "Agree or Disagree?" box. How can you help your church be more in tune with the AIDS issue? What would you like to see your church doing that it's not?

● If you knew a friend was involved in sex but wouldn't buy condoms, would you tell him to abstain, buy him condoms or not do anything? Explain.

● If you know someone's going to do something you don't agree with, is it better for you to ignore it or give advice on it? Explain.

● How do you make sexual decisions in your own life?

Special School for Gay Kids Sparks Controversy

NEW YORK—A special high school for gay boys and lesbian girls is in operation in New York City by the Institute for Protection of Lesbian and Gay Youth.

In an Institute survey, 20 percent of lesbians and 50 percent of gay men reported harassment or physical abuse. Harvey Milk School, which holds class sessions in a church, educates homosexual students who could not deal with public high school.

Joyce Hunter, director of the Institute, says, "In the schools, many of them were beaten up, humiliated and verbally abused." According to Nathan Quinones, head of the city's public schools, most of the students rarely went to their regular schools. Some dropped out and spent their time "cruising on the West Side of Manhattan ... selling themselves."

Dr. Lawrence Hartmann, a child psychiatry instructor at Harvard Medical School in Boston, is concerned that Harvey Milk School students may "prematurely decide that they have all the answers about their sexual identity." But he adds such schools are "psychiatrically safe and reasonable."

Dr. Felix Duang, school spokesperson for San Francisco, which has one of the largest concentrations of gays in the nation, said, "We try to mainstream students so that they have the experience of meeting boys and girls from all walks of life because that's what they're going to do when they graduate."

What's Your Reaction?

Draw the appropriate face (😊 , 😟 or 😕) after each statement. Give reasons for your reaction.

How would you feel if ...
- you saw someone at school who "looked and acted" like a homosexual?
- a close friend of the same sex told you he or she was a homosexual?
- you remained close friends with a homosexual?
- you were physically attracted to someone of the same sex?
- the person sitting next to you was a homosexual?
- two people of the same sex were affectionate in public?
- students harassed gays and lesbians at your school?
- a homosexual was a member of your church?
- a homosexual claimed to be a Christian?

Discussion Starters

● Should homosexual teenagers go to separate schools? Why or why not?

● How are homosexuals mistreated in public schools? Why are so many people cruel to homosexuals? What is it about a school for homosexuals that bothers some people?

● If a person is a homosexual and someone mistreats him or her, whose fault is it? Explain.

● If you were the superintendent of schools, how would you feel about opening schools for homosexuals? Would you vote for a separate school for homosexuals? Why or why not?

● Does opening a special school for homosexuals mean that being homosexual is okay? Why or why not? Can a teenager really know whether he or she will be a homosexual for life? Explain.

● How might separating homosexual teenagers from others lessen their chance of changing their sexual preference in the future?

● Read Romans 1:26-27 and 1 Corinthians 6:9-11. What message do these verses give homosexuals? Read 1 Corinthians 13:1-10. What message do these verses give? How can the messages be so different? Explain. Does God want people to condemn or love homosexuals? Explain.

● Read Galatians 5:19-21. Does a high school for homosexuals perpetuate immorality? Why or why not? Are teenagers using homosexuality as a reason to not get along with others? Explain.

● Read Galatians 5:22-25. Does opening a school for homosexuals show Christian love? Why or why not? Read Galatians 6:1-4, 8-10. How should Christians respond to homosexual teenagers? Are homosexuals members of the "family of believers"? Why or why not?

● How is opening a high school for homosexuals like or unlike opening a high school for sexually active heterosexuals?

● Do the "What's Your Reaction?" box. How would Jesus treat homosexuals?

● What would you tell a friend who thought he or she was homosexual?

Sex Ads Bring Big Bucks

NEW YORK—Paul Marciano is making a lot of money and creating a lot of heat—body heat and otherwise—by selling sex. And he says kids are buying it like it's never going out of style.

Marciano is co-founder and advertising director of Guess fashions. Guess sells clothes the "old-fashioned" way—with slick, expensive and sexually suggestive photos.

Guess ads have shown two women locked in a sensual embrace, two men and a woman in a suggestive position, and a man's hand opening a submissive-looking girl's blouse.

Wayne Maser, Marciano's photographer, says he tries to depict teenage life, including desires, needs and dreams. Is it working? You bet. Companies making designer jeans continue to set sales records across America.

Discussion Starters

● Is Paul Marciano's advertising objectionable? If so, what should be done about it? Should it be banned? Why or why not?

● If you aren't bothered by Marciano's advertising, would you be willing to pose for one of his ads? Why or why not?

● Do you think Marciano and his photographer are really experts on today's teenagers? Do the ads reflect your "desires, needs and dreams"? Why or why not? If not, why do Guess jeans sell by the millions to teenagers?

● Read Romans 12:1-2. Is buying these products conforming to this world? Explain. If bodies are God's creation, what can be wrong with portraying them in these ways?

● Read Colossians 3:17. What does this verse say about the models in these ads? Is posing for these ads a way of thanking God for beautiful bodies? Why or why not?

● Read 1 Corinthians 6:13 and 1 Thessalonians 4:3-5. How would the advertisers respond to these verses? the buyers? the models? the photographers? Explain.

● Read Philippians 4:8. What does this verse say that relates to sexually suggestive ads? What should your reaction be to the ads?

SECTION FIVE:
Law and Violence

Boyfriend Burns House; Four People Die in Fire

FORT COLLINS, Colo.—Early one July morning, Kathy D'Amelio and four friends were asleep in an upstairs apartment when the house was suddenly ablaze. Only one of the five escaped.

Before noon on the same day authorities arrested D'Amelio's former boyfriend, Gregory Bowers, 25. He was charged with first-degree murder.

Investigation showed that Bowers was extremely troubled over his breakup with D'Amelio six weeks before the fire. They had lived together for a year.

At the time of the breakup, Bowers "got angry and trashed the apartment," he later admitted to police. Kathy became frightened, moved to another apartment and kept the address a secret.

The night before the fire D'Amelio attended a party at a friend's apartment and trouble with Bowers began. It included tire-slashing and high-speed driving in front of the house. D'Amelio and her four friends went to bed.

According to Bowers, at about 2 a.m. he sprayed lighter fluid in the foyer and used his lighter to start the blaze. "I didn't mean to kill them, but to scare them. All I wanted was for Kathy to come back."

Anger Advice

Write key words from each verse that give advice about anger.

Proverbs 14:17 _____

Proverbs 15:1 _____

Proverbs 15:18 _____

Proverbs 22:24 _____

Proverbs 27:4 _____

Proverbs 29:22 _____

Ecclesiastes 7:9 _____

How can you use these words to help you handle anger constructively?

Discussion Starters

● What could have prevented this tragedy? What could Kathy D'Amelio have done to make the breakup easier? What could Gregory Bowers have done to better deal with his anger?

● When is anger dangerous? When is anger helpful? Why is it difficult to express anger? Is it okay for Christians to get angry? Why or why not?

● Do people most often get angry with people close to them or people they hardly know? Explain.

● How do you know when your anger has gone too far? Read Ephesians 4:26-27, 31-32 and Colossians 3:8. When does anger lead to sin?

● Do the "Anger Advice" box. What are healthy, practical ways to get rid of anger?

● Read Matthew 5:21-26. Is it always possible to follow these verses? Why or why not? Who's responsible for dealing with anger—the giver or the receiver? Explain.

● Read Jeremiah 7:16-20 and Nahum 1:2-7. Why is God angry? What kind of example does God set for us? What makes God angry?

● Think of a time when your anger got out of control and caused more damage than you intended. What can you do to prevent that in the future?

Father Shot; Children Charged With Murder

CHEYENNE, Wyo. — Two Cheyenne teenagers, being tried as adults, pleaded innocent to charges involving the ambush slaying of their father at the family's home north of Cheyenne.

Authorities alleged that Richard Jahnke, 16, and Deborah Jahnke, 17, decided to "execute" their father, 38-year-old Internal Revenue Service agent Richard Jahnke, following a family argument.

Richard was accused of firing the shots. Deborah allegedly waited inside the house with a .30-caliber carbine. Richard was charged with first-degree murder and conspiracy to commit murder. Deborah was charged with aiding and abetting a first-degree murder and conspiracy to commit murder.

The young teenagers' mother, Maria Jahnke, testified that $18\frac{1}{2}$ years of marriage to the slain man were filled with turmoil and violence directed against her and the two children. She said the father began beating Deborah when she was 4. She testified that the beatings continued on a regular basis until the father's death.

Mrs. Jahnke said she never sought help in dealing with the family situation because she was afraid of her husband. "[And] there was always the hope I could do something to solve the violence.

"I'm not glad he is dead. There's just not that tension, that fear that someone is going to be hurt. That screaming and degrading is not going to happen anymore," she said.

Discussion Starters

● How would you rule if you were a member of the jury? Should the children be charged with murdering their father? Or should they be released because their father abused them? Explain.

● If they're guilty, what should be their punishment? If they're innocent, should they be allowed to go completely free? Why or why not? How much abuse would it take for you to murder someone?

● Read Exodus 20:13. What do you think God would say to Richard Jahnke?

● Should the mother be punished for allowing her children to murder their father? Should she be punished for letting the father abuse the children? What would you do if you were the mother?

● Read Proverbs 21:15 and Matthew 23:23. What are the criteria for deciding what is "just" in this situation?

● Read Matthew 10:37-39; Luke 14:26-27; and Ephesians 6:1. Do parents have a right to do whatever they wish to their children—even abuse them? Why or why not? When is disobedience to parents justified, if ever?

● Are there times when parents abuse their authority? What can be done about constant abuse of authority? Read Romans 13:1-5. Can this advice apply to the parents' authority? Explain.

● What do you think God wants parents and children to do when problems come up? What outside resources do families have for help with problems?

● Read Ephesians 6:1-4. What responsibilities do family members have toward each other? List the ways you think people can express different levels of anger. Read Colossians 3:12-17. How could families build into their family life the qualities listed here? Match your suggested activities with each quality.

● List groups, organizations and people in your community and church who can help kids deal with abusive parents. List personal strengths, insights and beliefs that could help kids who feel overcontrolled or abused. How can you help develop those personal resources?

● Describe ways a person who isn't involved in a conflict can be helpful to those who are.

Weapons Discovered in Schools; Kids Arrested

NEW YORK—Police arrested an 18-year-old Manhattan young person at New York's East Side Junior High School after he was found with a loaded Uzi submachine gun. The arrest was not an isolated incident. In one year, more than 1,500 weapons were seized inside New York schools. The problem is so widespread that school district chancellor Richard Green has threatened to install metal detectors in every school to keep the weapons out.

In Detroit, one middle-schooler and 14 high-schoolers were permanently expelled for carrying weapons. School district officials responded by randomly installing metal detectors in many schools.

"It's real unfortunate that we've come to that level," said Ron Garrison, the National School Safety Center's field services director. Because of the violence, "the more competent teachers are saying, 'Hey, I didn't get into this [teaching] to get shot at.' So teachers are leaving simply because it [the classroom] is not a safe place to be."

Despite the growing problem with weapons, many school administrators don't think metal detectors are the answer. Reuben Trinidad, principal of San Jose's Overfelt High School, says, "I just don't think that it [a metal detector] is the right approach." Overfelt administrators turned their school around by removing lockers that served as a storage area for guns and drugs, "then showing the kids going to Overfelt that it's a safe place to be ... You are going to be treated as a human being and we expect you to treat teachers and other students with the same respect."

Discussion Starters

● If kids at your school are bringing weapons to class, is it a good idea to install a metal detector at every door? Why or why not? Should school officials have the right to search your locker if they believe you're hiding weapons or drugs? Why or why not?

● Read Psalm 23:4. If you were a teacher, would you continue teaching in a school that has a weapons problem? Why or why not?

● Read Matthew 5:39. If someone at school threatened you with a weapon, would you get a weapon to protect yourself? Why or why not? Why are the students bringing weapons to class?

● Read Matthew 5:43-48. If Jesus was a student at a school with a weapons problem, what would he do about it? What's the most difficult thing about responding to our enemies the way Jesus wants us to? Read Matthew 26:47-52. Is Jesus saying it's always wrong to carry a weapon? Explain. Why didn't Jesus use a weapon to protect himself from the soldiers?

● Read 1 Samuel 17:31-40. Why was David confident he could defeat Goliath? When David decided not to use Saul's armor or weapons, what did he receive from the Lord instead?

● How can you help stop violence in your school without using weapons?

● Read Matthew 5:9. Why are "peacemakers" called the "sons of God"? Read Matthew 12:35. If school officials made sure no one brought weapons to school, would that solve the violence problem? Why or why not?

Christians Arrested for Abortion Clinic Bombings

RELIGIOUS NEWS SERVICE PHOTO

One leading abortion opponent considers abortion "America's blood sacrifice to convenience, pride and having our own way."

Bombings
Bombing an abortion clinic is most like . . .
(Circle your answer and give reasons for it.)

WASHINGTON—The president of the National Organization for Women called it "terrorist activity." The Assemblies of God general superintendent said: "We do not support this kind of activity. We do not believe violence is the way to express convictions on any moral issue." Yet anti-abortion bombings continue.

Three Maryland men arrested in eight anti-abortion bombings are considered hard-working family men and devout Christians. The men were suspected in the bombings of abortion clinics, a Planned Parenthood office, the National Abortion Federation and an American Civil Liberties Union office.

Discussion Starters

● How is bombing an abortion clinic like "terrorist activity"? How do you feel about the statement that abortion is "America's blood sacrifice to convenience, pride and having our own way"? Do you agree? Explain.

● Why do devout Christians bomb abortion clinics?

● Who is more wrong—the bombers, the women getting abortions or the people who perform abortions? Explain.

● If people strongly oppose an issue, what's the best way to get their opinion heard?

● If people oppose abortion because they're against innocent human beings getting killed, how can they bomb innocent people near abortion clinics and have a clear conscience? Explain. Who're the victims in abortion clinic bombings?

● Should women have the right to go to abortion clinics in peace? Why or why not? What if angry people started bombing buildings representing everything they opposed, such as traffic laws, high prices, chemical wastes?

● Read Exodus 20:13. In the case of abortion clinic bombings, who's the killer? Why? Read Matthew 5:38-42. How does this apply to abortion clinic bombings? Should people oppose violence with violence? Explain.

● Read Matthew 18:15-17. What's the proper way to confront someone you feel has sinned? How could this apply to abortion clinic bombings?

● Read James 2:14-18. How are Christian abortion clinic bombers showing their faith? Are the abortion clinic bombings a sign of strong or weak faith? Explain.

● Read Ecclesiastes 3:1-3. Are abortions ever right? Why or why not? Are abortion clinic bombings ever right? Why or why not? Who decides when it's time to kill or heal? Why?

● Do the "Bombings" box. What should your Christian response be to abortion clinic bombers? to abortion clinics? to women who've had abortions? to someone who wants an abortion?

New Law Would Punish Parents for Kids' Crimes

LOS ANGELES—Should parents be punished for their kids' crimes?

That's a controversial question in California, where Los Angeles police arrested the mother of a 17-year-old rape suspect and gang member.

Gloria Williams is the 37-year-old mother of a Crips gang member who police suspect helped rape a 12-year-old girl. Police arrested Williams using a precedent-setting California law that holds parents responsible for their children's crimes.

Some say the law is not only unfair, it's unworkable.

"The idea behind the California law is that parents should rein in their children like dog owners should rein in bull terriers," says Melvin Guyer, a lawyer and associate professor of psychiatry at University of Michigan Hospitals. "It's cosmetic, hasty legislation that will have no positive effect and, in my view, may make the problem worse."

Federal drug czar William Bennett disagrees. He says, "Parents who have effectively turned [juvenile offenders] loose must learn why the social contract demands that they oversee and control the impulses of their children."

When police entered Williams' apartment to talk about her son, they found walls covered with gang graffiti. Her photo albums showed family members pointing guns. A birthday cake for her 8-year-old was decorated with the gang name.

Bob Sardelli of Key Solutions, a Michigan group for parents of children in trouble, says: "The problem is our society today, where everything is so permissive and parents' time with children is so limited because they have to make a living."

Discussion Starters

● How do you feel about the California law that makes parents responsible for their kids' crimes? If a friend of yours commits a crime and you do nothing about it, are you partially responsible for the crime? Why or why not? How much responsibility should your parents have for your actions?

● Read Proverbs 22:6. How do you "train a child in the way he should go"? Do you think Gloria Williams followed this advice? Explain. How likely is it that kids who've been negatively "trained" will continue down the wrong path in life? Explain. Will kids who've been positively "trained" probably continue down the right path? Why or why not?

● Read Proverbs 23:12-14. Is discipline more loving or more hurtful? Explain. If you had children, what would your discipline policy be?

● Read John 9:1-7 and Ephesians 6:4. How can the sins of parents affect their children? In your opinion, when a son or daughter commits a crime, what percentage of the blame falls on the parents? If a child has irresponsible, hurtful parents, can God give that child what the parents didn't? Why or why not? Does God hold parents accountable for their kids' mistakes? Explain.

● Read Matthew 10:34-37 and Ephesians 6:1-3. Describe a time when it was hard to obey God and your parents at the same time. Is it ever okay to disobey your parents? Why or why not? At what age should young people be responsible for their own actions? Explain.

Killer of Homosexuals Given Light Sentence

DALLAS—A judge stirred controversy within the Dallas religious community when he handed a convicted killer a light sentence because the victims were homosexual.

District judge Jack Hampton said he sentenced 18-year-old Richard Lee Bednarski to 30 years in prison instead of the maximum life sentence in part because the two murder victims were "queers."

Hampton said he "put prostitutes and gays at about the same level" and would be "hard put to give somebody life for killing a prostitute."

The remarks stirred the gay community, equal rights activists and church leaders to protest and seek Hampton's removal from the bench.

Ken Coulter, pastor of Grace Fellowship Church and part of a coalition of church leaders who minister to large numbers of gays, said Hampton's remarks may mean "open season" on homosexuals.

Meanwhile, Rev. Don Skelton, pastor of Fountain of the Living Word, said at least seven pastors agreed to take part in a support rally for Hampton outside the courthouse. He expected 100 to 150 people to attend.

"We're very much opposed to sodomy," Skelton says. "It's against Texas law for one thing and God's law for another thing." Sodomy carries up to a $200 fine in Texas.

Discussion Starters

● Are you for or against the remarks made by the judge? Explain. Do homosexuals and prostitutes have less value in society because of their lifestyles? Why or why not?

● Read Leviticus 18:22; 20:13; and Romans 1:22-28. What does God think of homosexuals? Do people choose to be homosexual, or are they born that way? Explain. Does God love homosexuals as much as he loves heterosexuals? Why or why not?

● Read Proverbs 28:21; Romans 2:1-11; and 3:23. If all sin is detestable to God, is it right to say homosexuality is worse than other sins? Why or why not? How is the way the courts judge people different from the way God judges them? How does "God's kindness" lead to repentance?

● Read John 8:1-11. By letting the woman go, did Jesus overlook her sin? Why or why not? If the woman sinned, why didn't Jesus agree to give her the normal penalty for adultery?

● Read Micah 6:6-8. What's your definition of justice? What's God's definition of justice? How well did Judge Hampton fulfill either definition? Explain.

● Read 2 Corinthians 5:21. How were Jesus' struggles with sin similar to or different from your struggles? If we sin, what's the only way we can stand pure before God? If you thought you might be gay, what would you do?

Mother Arrested for Humiliating Her Child

HAYWARD, Calif.—Police charged a woman with child abuse after she punished her 7-year-old son for stealing by painting his face blue, tying his hands behind his back, taping a cardboard pig's snout to his face and hanging a sign on his chest that read, "I'm a dumb pig."

The boy was tied to a bench in his front yard, where neighbors watched him cry for 30 minutes. The mother, 29-year-old Mary Francis Bergamasco, told police she was practicing the kind of discipline her own mother used. Police say Bergamasco told them she was punishing her son for a two-week stealing spree. The boy's haul included $25 worth of baseball cards, $6 in cash and other small items.

Bergamasco said she wanted her son to understand "for if only 30 minutes that lying and stealing make you ugly like Pinocchio." She added that her punishment may have been wrong, but "Mom said it worked on us kids."

Craig Hoyer, a child abuse investigator for the Hayward Police Department, said: "This is a first for me. This was public humiliation. When your peers see you like that, in my mind, it could almost destroy a kid's psyche."

Bergamasco was arrested for misdemeanor child abuse and released on her own recognizance. Her two children, including the boy, were put in protective custody.

Discussion Starters

● Should parents have the right to punish their children any way they want, as long as they don't physically abuse them? Why or why not? If you were a parent and caught your son or daughter stealing, what punishment would you choose? Is it all right to punish someone in front of others, or should it be done privately? Explain your answer.

● If you were one of the boy's neighbors and saw him crying in his front yard, what would you do? call the police? untie the boy from the bench? talk to the mother? Do you think the boy's psyche was damaged by his punishment? Why or why not?

● Read Hebrews 12:5-11. In what ways does God discipline us? How does God show his love for us through his discipline? If God never disciplined you, how would you feel? If your parents never disciplined you, how would you feel? Explain.

● Verse 11 says that those who are trained by discipline yield "a harvest of righteousness and peace." What is "a harvest of righteousness" and how can discipline train you to produce it? How is the way God disciplines you different from the way your parents discipline you?

● Read 2 Samuel 1:2-16. Why did David punish the messenger with death? Was death a proper punishment under the circumstances, or did David overreact? Explain. What right did David have to discipline the messenger? What right do your parents have to discipline you?

● Read Luke 2:41-52. Do you think Jesus disobeyed his parents? Why or why not? Should Joseph and Mary have disciplined Jesus for staying in Jerusalem after they left? Why or why not? Have you ever wandered away and gotten lost when you were with your parents? How did they react when they found you? How did you feel?

● Read Ephesians 4:28. Using the verse as a guide, write what you think is a fair and just punishment for stealing.

● Read John 8:1-11. Hebrew law says a woman caught in adultery should be stoned to death. Was Jesus breaking his own law by letting the woman go? Why or why not? How does Jesus' decision in this situation make you feel? Why do you think Jesus stooped down and wrote on the ground before he answered the scribes and Pharisees? What does Jesus' reaction to the woman's sin tell you about the way God disciplines? Make believe you're a parent, and write three principles of godly discipline you would use with your kids.

SECTION SIX:
Unusual Stories

Elvis Worshiped by Fans

MEMPHIS, Tenn.—Hundreds of people claim he's spoken to them from the afterlife. More than 500,000 adoring fans visit his home every year. And 10,000 followers hold a candlelight vigil to commemorate the day he died. Elvis Presley is more than a deceased singer to his adoring fans. He's a religious icon.

Presley died on August 16, 1977. Or did he? In her book *Is Elvis Alive?* Gail Brewer-Giorgio makes the claim that Elvis never died. She says one clue to Elvis' resurrection is found at his grave site in Memphis. Elvis' real middle name is spelled Aron, but the name on his gravestone reads Aaron. Brewer-Giorgio's conclusion: Elvis *Aron* Presley is not buried there.

"This has the makings of the rise of a new religion," says the Rev. Robert D. Martin, a retired Episcopal minister. "Elvis is the god, and Graceland (Elvis' home) the shrine. There are no writings, but that could be his music. And some even say he is rising again. The August week is more like people going to Lourdes than to an entertainment event. People genuflect before his grave. Women have come to Memphis to deliver babies, claiming Elvis is the father and that he will come down from heaven when the boy is 16 to anoint him—sort of like Jesus in the Jordan River."

Officials in charge of Elvis' estate have quickly capitalized on "the King's" post-mortem popularity. The estate's assets are now valued at $50 million, 10 times the amount listed at his death.

Rate Your Hero

Write the name of your hero below. Then give that person a rating from 1 to 10 (1=not at all; 10=very much) on each of the hero qualities taken from biblical heroes such as Jonathan, David, Stephen, Paul and Jesus.

Your hero's name:	Rating
Makes bold, selfless decisions	1 2 3 4 5 6 7 8 9 10
Is willing to admit wrong actions or decisions	1 2 3 4 5 6 7 8 9 10
Trusts God more than own intuition or others' advice	1 2 3 4 5 6 7 8 9 10
Not afraid to risk death to do what is right	1 2 3 4 5 6 7 8 9 10
Not afraid to praise goodness and expose evil or wrongdoing	1 2 3 4 5 6 7 8 9 10
Isn't afraid to look foolish for a good cause	1 2 3 4 5 6 7 8 9 10
Knows when to talk and when to be silent	1 2 3 4 5 6 7 8 9 10
Doesn't seek revenge even when wronged	1 2 3 4 5 6 7 8 9 10
Cares more about inward characteristics than outward characteristics	1 2 3 4 5 6 7 8 9 10

Discussion Starters

● Read 2 Thessalonians 3:7-9. Paul said it was okay to follow his example. How do you feel about people who follow Elvis?

● Read Exodus 20:1-6. What are modern-day idols our society worships? If you're a fan of someone, how is that the same as or different from worship? Is it possible to worship a star and worship God at the same time? Why or why not?

● Read 2 Timothy 2:22-23 and Titus 3:9. Is it a waste of time to read books and articles that try to prove Elvis is still alive? Why are people so fascinated with Elvis? Do you think the people who go to a candlelight service honoring Elvis are "foolish and ignorant"? Why or why not? If someone tried to convince you Elvis is still alive, how would you respond?

● Read Acts 17:24-29. Why do some people worship Elvis and not God? If Elvis had never died, how would people's reverence of him be different? Some people today say they've heard Elvis talking to them in their dreams, comforting and giving them instructions. Is it possible that Elvis is really talking to these people? Why or why not?

● Read Romans 1:21-25 and Galatians 4:8-9. Is it possible to really know God, yet not worship him? Why or why not? Why is it hard for some people to accept the words of Jesus, but easy for them to study and revere the words of Elvis? What happens to your heart when you worship a creature instead of the Creator?

● Read Acts 10:22-26. Why did Cornelius bow down before Peter? Do you think Peter was tempted to let Cornelius worship him? Why or why not? What's the difference between honoring someone and worshiping someone?

● Do the "Rate Your Hero" box. Is it good to have heros? Why or why not?

Report Claims Men Can Now Become Pregnant

LONDON—The news: Men can give birth, according to a report in the British weekly magazine New Society.

The report says the technology now exists for men to carry fetuses to development. "And undoubtedly someone will do it," said Dr. John Parsons of King's College Hospital in London.

For a man to become pregnant, a donated egg would be fertilized with sperm outside of the body. The resulting embryo would be implanted into the man's abdomen, where it could attach itself to a kidney or the large intestine.

The pregnant man would need to receive hormone treatments to stimulate normal prenatal changes, such as the formation of a placenta. The baby would have to be born through surgery.

People most likely to take advantage of this new technology are homosexuals, transsexuals or men whose wives are infertile, New Society speculates.

Who'd Do It?

If men begin giving birth, I think those most likely to do so are ... (checkmark your answers)

- homosexuals._____
- single men._____
- transsexuals._____
- men whose wives are infertile._____
- men whose wives don't want to get pregnant._____
- other:_____.

Discuss your feelings about each category of men giving birth. If you approve of some but not others, tell why.

Discussion Starters

● How does this article make you feel?

● Why do you think God planned for women but not men to bear babies? If science now has made it possible for men to have children, does that mean God approves? Why or why not?

● Would it ever be a good choice for a man to bear a child? Explain.

● If a man is unemployed and his wife has a high-paying job, would you approve of the couple's decision for the man to bear the child? Why or why not?

● Read 1 Corinthians 11:11-12. What does it mean for men and women to be dependent on each other? If "man is born of woman" changes to a "man is born of man," does that take away men's need for women?

● Read 1 Timothy 2:13-15. What does Paul mean that "women will be saved through childbearing"? How would this be affected if men begin bearing children?

● In John 3:3-8, Jesus tells Nicodemus it's the spiritual birth that's important, not the physical birth. Do you think it matters to God which parent's body a child develops in? Explain. Is it wrong for a man to have a baby since the baby would have to be delivered through surgery? Why or why not?

● What should your Christian response be to a pregnant man? How would you respond to a child whose "mom" was a man?

● What message would you give the world concerning the role of men and women in the birth process?

● Do the "Who'd Do It?" box.

Company Helps People Get Even With Enemies

NEWTON, Mass.—If you're a spurned lover or a frustrated employee, Nan Berman has some advice for you: Don't get mad, get even. Berman has a business called Enough Is Enough, billed as "Creative Revenge for Today's World." Berman has mailed a 3-foot dead bluefish to an unfaithful husband in California and delivered a burned and messy suit to a lawyer who implied his girlfriend was "unsuitable."

The most common requests, however, are for 13 dead roses sent in a black box ($25) and 13 black balloons tied together by a single black rose ($30). Other "insults to suit the occasion" include a real stuffed shirt ($25) for pompous employers and drinking glasses with cigarette butts on the bottom for smokers.

Berman says: "Twenty years ago, people didn't speak up the way they do now. But since the '60s, people have expressed themselves. With me, you really have a way to vent things out."

The 43-year-old Berman started Enough Is Enough after she spent a year driving a florist delivery truck for a boss who was "the grumpiest, most unpleasant person ever born."

Berman promises her customers anonymity. "I want to stress that we'll do anything, as long as it's legal," she says.

Discussion Starters

● Has someone taken revenge on you? Explain. How would you feel about using Berman's service?

● Read Exodus 21:23-25; Matthew 5:38-48; and Luke 6:27-36. When someone wrongs you, is your first reaction to demand an eye for an eye or do you turn the other cheek? Explain.

● Berman says her business gives people a "way to vent things out." Is this a healthy or unhealthy "vent" for anger? Explain.

● Is it realistic for human beings to love their enemies? Why or why not? Jesus said we're supposed to be "perfect, therefore, as your heavenly Father is perfect." What kind of perfection is Jesus talking about?

● Read John 8:1-11. Who did the adulterous woman hurt by her actions? Who was the only one in the crowd with a true "right of revenge"? How do you feel about Jesus' response to the situation? Since the woman wasn't punished, will she commit adultery again? Why or why not?

● Read Luke 9:51-56. What was the disciples' attitude toward their enemies? Why did Jesus rebuke them? Does Berman's business oppose God's Spirit? Why or why not? What would Jesus have done with the unfaithful husband in California?

● Read Romans 5:10. Are you an enemy or a friend of God right now? If God operated according to the goals of Enough Is Enough, what would be different about your life? When you hurt God by your actions, does he ever take revenge on you? Why or why not? What's the difference between revenge and discipline? Explain.

● Read Jeremiah 11:18-20. Was Jeremiah right for asking God to take vengeance on his enemies? Why or why not? Are you taking revenge when you ask God to deal with your enemies? Why or why not?

Couple Married After They Die in Plane Crash

TALLAHASSEE, Fla.—Mike and Toni, who were planning to get married, died in a single-engine plane crash. But the couple was married anyway.

Their pastor, Rev. Rayburn Blair of Temple Baptist Church, performed a wedding ceremony for the dead couple in front of 350 mourners before he began their funeral service.

The couple, Mike Ellis, 27, and Toni Goff, 23, had met with Blair for premarital counseling two weeks prior to the accident. "I'm perfectly at ease in performing this ceremony of holy matrimony," Blair said, "because I heard them already say yes."

Discussion Starters

● How did this article make you feel?

● How do you feel about the pastor's decision to marry Mike and Toni? Would they have wanted to be married even though they were dead? Why or why not?

● Why did the pastor marry Mike and Toni? Are they better off being married even though they're dead? Explain.

● The pastor said he heard Mike and Toni "already say yes." What did he mean? What are ways people say yes to marriage?

● By marrying a dead couple, did the pastor lower or elevate the meaning of marriage? Explain.

● What's more important: having a wedding or living out a marriage? Explain. Is just "being married" what matters? Why or why not?

● What would someone married one year say is important in a marriage? someone married five years? 20 years? Explain.

● Read Ecclesiastes 9:10. Do Mike and Toni know they got married? Why or why not? Read Ephesians 5:22-28. How can Mike and Toni's relationship meet these standards if they're dead?

● Read Matthew 22:23-30. If there won't be marriage in heaven, what was the point of Mike and Toni getting married at their funeral? Read Matthew 22:31-32 and Romans 7:2. Do you think Mike and Toni were ever married in God's eyes? What difference would it make, either way?

● How would you feel about attending a wedding-funeral?

● If you were planning to be married and you and your fiance/fiancee died, would you want to be married at your funeral? Explain.

● If only you died, would you want to be married? if only your fiance/fiancee died? Explain.

Fake Slings and Neck Braces Gain Sympathy

Fake arm slings and neck braces are hot items. And Quik Curt's Casual Casts, the mail-order business selling them, promises "Dozens of dates!" and "Sympathy Galore!" for people who use them.

Curtis Colligan began his fake-injuries business after observing two girls wearing casts in a ski lodge. Colligan said, "Every person who came in went over to talk to them, whether they knew these girls or not."

The sympathy-inducing items come complete with slogans like "I Ski Moguls" and "Married Life is Rough." The slings and casts are inexpensive and are "good for everything except medical use."

How are sales? The orders are piled up, waiting to be filled, according to Colligan.

How Do You Respond?

When you see the following items on people, how do you respond? Write your answers.

Discussion Starters

● How does the success of the fake-injuries business make you feel?

● Is wearing a fake arm sling being deceitful or just having fun? Explain. If a shy person uses a fake arm sling to get other people to start conversations with him or her, is that okay? Why or why not?

● What's wrong about feeling sorry for someone? What good is there in feeling sorry for someone? Is it okay to want sympathy? Why or why not?

● What are other ways people get sympathy? What have you done to get sympathy? How do some people take advantage of sympathy? Have you ever taken advantage of someone's sympathy? If so, why? How did the situation turn out?

● Read Luke 9:11. Why did people go to Jesus? How did he respond to them? Do you think people ever faked sickness to get close to Jesus? If so, how is that like faking an injury to start new relationships?

● Read Matthew 25:36. How does Jesus say we should treat sick people? What about people who pretend to be sick? Read Mark 2:17. What does Jesus say about people who aren't sick? If someone wears a fake cast, what is that person's real need?

● Read Psalm 103:8, 13. If *God* has mercy and pity for all people, should *we*? Why or why not? When you see people who seem sick or injured, how should you respond to them? If you know someone is faking an injury or illness, how should you respond?

● Do the "How Do You Respond?" box. Compare your answers with a friend's. What did you discover?

● Would you order a fake arm sling? Why or why not?

More Ministry-Building Resources

10-Minute Devotions for Youth Groups
By J.B. Collingsworth

Get this big collection of ready-to-use devotion ideas that'll help teenagers apply God's Word to their lives. Each 10-minute faith-building devotion addresses an important concern such as:

- love
- failure
- faith, and more
- peer pressure
- rejection

You'll get 52 quick devotions complete with scripture reference, attention-grabbing learning experience, discussion questions and a closing. Bring teenagers closer to God with these refreshing devotions—perfect for youth activities of any kind.

ISBN 0-931529-85-9 $6.95

Do It! Active Learning in Youth Ministry
By Thom and Joani Schultz

This practical resource will help you involve your teenagers in group meetings and activities—with creative non-lecture programming. You'll learn to design simple, fun programs that group members will look forward to ... and remember afterward. Plus, you'll get 24 ready-made, faith-building active-learning programs.

ISBN 0-931529-94-8 $9.95

Building Attendance in Your Youth Ministry
By Scott C. Noon

Now you can make your group grow—and learn what to do when it does! You'll get practical ideas for bringing new kids in the door, and design faith-building programs to keep them. Discover ...

- Formulas for setting realistic goals
- Hints for planning long-term expansion
- Effective ways to handle growth

Whether you're just starting out or a youth ministry veteran, you'll get tools that really work—for building attendance in *your* youth group!

ISBN 0-931529-84-0 $10.95

Creative Resources for Your Youth Ministry

Clown Ministry

By Floyd Shaffer and Penne Sewall

Discover how you can have an effective, successful clown ministry. Novice and pro alike will find practical, hands-on tips for ...

- Costumes
- Scripting
- Props and makeup
- Mime techniques
- Developing a clown character
- Organizing a clown group

Plus, you'll get 30 detailed skits and more than 50 short clowning bits.

ISBN 0936-664-18-5 $8.95

Creative Worship in Youth Ministry

By Dennis C. Benson

Involve your group in meaningful worship. Discover hundreds of colorful, creative ready-to-use worship ideas to help you ...

- Expand your group's understanding of worship
- Discover biblical background for all parts of worship
- Create meaningful, contemporary worship

Offer spiritual depth to your youth group with preplanned retreats, camps, youth Sundays, youth meetings, worship for holidays and much more. Use this idea packed resource today.

ISBN 0-931529-05-0 $11.95

Quick Skits & Discussion Starters

By Chuck Bolte and Paul McCusker

Here's a new tool for grabbing attention and building faith in youth groups. Help your teenagers build confidence and self-esteem. Improve communication skills. Practice teamwork. And examine issues from a Christian perspective. You'll get complete instructions, 26 simple warm-up exercises, 18 quick skits and thought-provoking discussion questions with matching biblical references.

ISBN 0-931529-68-9 $9.95

Solid Support for Your Volunteers

Volunteer Training Series:
Youth Ministry Essentials

By Walt Marcum

Now you can equip your adult volunteers with practical youth ministry skills. Help your volunteers answer these tough questions . . .

- Am I qualified to work with teenagers?
- How can I be an effective youth worker?
- What do kids really need from a volunteer?
- How can I be part of the team?

It's easy to train volunteers with six ready-to-use sessions, each including clear objectives. Handy preparation tips. And complete, step-by-step outlines.

Boost the confidence of your volunteers. Provide encouragement. And build a close-knit team of enthused, qualified youth workers.

Paperback   ISBN 1-55945-012-6 $8.95

Volunteer Training Series:
Youth Ministry Leadership Skills

By Scott C. Noon

Develop the leadership potential of your adult volunteers. You'll get six complete, in-depth training sessions to help volunteers learn to . . .

- Guide teenagers in lively, meaningful discussions
- Speak in front of young people—with confidence
- Lead a successful large group event
- Deal constructively with group disruptions
- Give teenagers responsibility they can handle

Each ready-to-use session includes clear objectives, handy preparation tips and step-by-step outlines. Nurture the leadership gifts of your adult volunteers.

Paperback   ISBN 1-55945-013-4 $8.95

These and other Group products are available at your local Christian bookstore. Or order direct from the publisher. Write Group, Box 481, Loveland, CO 80539. Please add $3 for postage/handling per order. Colorado residents add 3% sales tax.